W9-BFT-574

THE *Personal* TOUCH

THE Personal TOUCH

What You Really Need to Succeed in Today's Fast-paced Business World

TERRIE WILLIAMS

with Joe Cooney

Foreword by
BILL COSBY

Preface by
JONATHAN TISCH

A Time Warner Company

Warner Books, Inc., 1271 Avenue of the Americas, New York, NY 10020

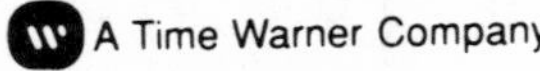

Printed in the United States of America
First Printing: September 1994
10 9 8 7 6 5 4 3 2 1

Library of Congress Cataloging-in-Publication Data

Williams, Terrie.
The personal touch : what you really need to succeed in today's fast-paced business world / Terrie Williams with Joe Cooney.
p. cm.
ISBN 0-446-51775-5
1. Success in business. 2. Williams, Terrie. 3. Terrie Williams Agency—Case studies. I. Cooney, Joe. II. Title.
HF5386.W555 1994
650.1—dc20 94-9123
CIP

Book design by Giorgetta Bell McRee

To my grandmother, Lady D.
I miss you.

Table of Contents

Foreword

About seven years ago, Arthur Ashe and I were talking about being in the public eye and about how people treated us—as celebrities—with a certain amount of respect. And as Arthur and I continued talking, we agreed that we wanted to make sure our children realized that respect goes beyond the realm of celebrity. Everyone—celebrity or not—deserves a certain esteem.

Terrie Williams has become a success because she knows how to deal with people, and she knows how to treat everyone with respect. It's something that Terrie does very, very well. To be able to understand and handle human behavior—and then apply that "personal touch" at work—requires a person who is listening, who is way ahead, who is respectful. Terrie Williams is that person.

This behavior should be applied to dealing with people in any form of business and in any walk of life. Terrie happens to be in the business of celebrity management and publicity. It is a very difficult business because some celebrities, even though they are treated with respect, sometimes fail to return that respect to others. For example: There's a time set for a particular press event for a performer. Said performer knows they have to be there at ten. The car is waiting, and all arrangements have been made, but the performer still keeps everyone waiting. The performer finally arrives—fifty minutes late. Terrie, who has already soothed the waiting press, now has to approach the performer and, in a very short amount of time, get them to get their act together, turn on the charm, and go in there and be very nice. What does Terrie say? How does she put it to that person? I don't know. But I do know that it requires genius. Some people will say that it requires "mother wit." But I think that a mother would just slap that person. So that wit is out.

In the case of Terrie, though, I think we're looking at someone who has the abilities of a behavioral scientist. A person who knows how to put a soothing philosophical ointment on something that requires massaging at moments like this. Which means, in many instances, Terrie has saved an awful lot of careers. There are people who probably will never know how, or why, their careers are still going. But Terrie knows: it has to do with respect.

This book is something that Terrie is willing to share with you. It will help you become a better person—it may even boost your career. You can only thank Terrie for writing this book. But knowing her, I know she had to do it. It has nothing to do with "mother wit." It just has to do with the fact that she cares about people.

—Bill Cosby

Preface

Since first meeting Terrie in 1988 when I was chairing the New York City Host Committee for the Grammy Awards, I have come to admire her achievement in building one of the country's most successful entertainment public relations agencies. Yet, while I respect her entrepreneurial spirit and business savvy, it is her commitment to people, and to giving something back to help others, that has made a lasting impression on me.

At Loews Hotels we have always reflected a similar philosophy. Our Good Neighbor Policy allows us to respond to the issues and concerns of the people who live and work in the communities where our hotels are located. Just as Terrie has always demonstrated by her actions and deeds, and as she so appropriately points out in this book, we understand that adding a human, personal touch is the key to success, especially in today's hectic and often dispassionate business world.

As a role model and mentor, Terrie has the vision and commitment to inspire those looking to begin or advance their own careers. Anyone who wants to become a better person and a bigger success should follow the lead of Terrie Williams. This book will show you how.

—Jonathan M. Tisch,
President and CEO, Loews Hotels

THE *Personal* TOUCH

Introduction

On February 1, 1988, the legal documents and the incorporation papers were signed, and The Terrie Williams Agency, a full-service public relations, marketing, and communications firm, officially began doing business.

I started my own company—geared initially to handle personal publicity for entertainers and celebrities—by signing two of the biggest names in the world even before I officially opened the doors: Eddie Murphy, the internationally known box office champion and king of comedic actors; and Miles Davis, a true legend of music and one of the most influential jazz artists the world has ever known. The list of clients steadily grew, and within the first year we also represented Grammy Award–winning songstress Anita Baker, Olympic gold medalist Jackie Joyner-Kersee, and Essence Communications, Inc., one of the largest and fastest-growing Black-owned communications firms in the country.

Over the years, the Agency has diversified into all areas of public relations and marketing. We have consistently worked with the foremost entertainers, sports stars, film companies, business corporations, publishing houses, authors, and political figures. The names on our roster have included Bobby Brown, Janet Jackson, Hammer, Martin Lawrence, Dawnn Lewis, Matty Rich, Russell Simmons, Sinbad, Wesley Snipes, major league baseball star Dave Winfield, moviemakers Warrington and Reginald Hudlin, and Washington, D.C., Mayor Sharon Pratt Kelly. We've represented corporations as well, including GRP Records, The Disney Channel, HBO, Miramax Films, New Line Cinema, Tribune Entertainment, and the Samuel Goldwyn Company. There has been AT&T, Consolidated Edison, Coca-Cola Bottling Company of New York, Laurel Entertainment, Polaroid, RUSH Communications, Time Warner, Harcourt Brace & Company, Harper/Collins Publishers, Little, Brown & Company, and Simon & Schuster.

The Agency has been called "the most powerful Black-owned public relations firm in the country." Each year we continue to grow and expand our client base, and we're on our way to ranking right up there among *all* of the nation's PR firms—not solely minority-owned companies. I'm looking to break into the top list of the Jack O'Dwyer's *Directory of Public Relations Firms* (the bible of public relations firms).

Believe it or not—but I'm telling you that it is a fact—I had no agency experience whatsoever when I opened the doors to my company. None. And it was done without benefit of the established old boy/old girl network. *And* I didn't have any money. What I did have was a unique formula for success that combines a distinctive work ethic—involving attention to detail, drive, determination, honesty, and integrity—with a way of life that revolves around the fact that *we are all human beings*. You will see that my philosophy is based on lots of different factors and elements, but it all stems basically from one main point: We are on this planet to support one another as human beings, first, last, and always. That is my credo, my doctrine, my motto. I have proven time and again throughout my career that it's possible to achieve more and to be more successful by adhering to this basic premise.

We are in a high-tech, fast-paced world that is all too often alienating and impersonal. We don't talk to people anymore when doing our banking, our shopping, our researching. We talk to machines. Competitive businesspeople try to maintain an edge by enhancing their skills in such nonpersonal areas as database management, desktop publishing, and information research. And that's fine. But you still need an edge. What is going to separate you or your company from competitors with the same capabilities and skills? You need something more. You need a personal touch.

When you get right down to it, and when all is said and done, it is how you connect with people on a human, personal level that will ensure your success. Relationships are key. Understanding and knowing the people you are dealing with is important. And above all, your everyday thoughts and actions should be kind, compassionate, and filled with good intentions. Know that the measure you give is the measure you receive.

This book shows you how to apply a unique way of dealing with people (on a personal and a professional level) that will enhance your image, broaden people's awareness of you, and enable you to achieve an extraordinary level of success—in life as well as in whatever vocation you choose. Whether you are just starting out, looking to change careers, jump-starting a stalled career, or just looking to improve the path you are on, this book will show you the best way to get from point A to point B and to stand out while you're doing it.

I have been blessed with many successes, and I have always believed strongly that with success comes responsibility. One of my passions and main obligations is to "give back" what I have learned and experienced, and that is one reason I have written this book. I also speak regularly before various groups, write articles, and offer my time and experiences with individuals—to share how I have accomplished some of the things I have—and to show how anyone else with commitment can, too.

I know my message is getting out there, and I know it's working for others. Not a day goes by without my receiving a letter, a handwritten note, or a phone call from someone who mentions the benefits of employing these methods. A single mother in Detroit has my "20 points" of marketing yourself (published in *Essence* magazine in 1988—a copy of which can be found at the back of this book) taped on her refrigerator as encouragement and plans to follow those guidelines when she heads back into the business world. A young professional who attended one of my speaking engagements sent me a thank-you note for taking the time to speak with her personally after my presentation. Another young woman wrote to say how stunned she was that I remembered her name after a brief introduction and that I responded personally to her request for information. A seasoned press photographer called to compliment us on the "extra-special" job we did at a movie premiere we handled. And, of course, my clients often thank me, even when their loyalty is thanks enough.

I must admit that it's weird to me that I even get stopped on the street by people who recognize my face from articles written on me and my company. Most of them are folks just wanting to say hello or young people who have followed my career, eager to share their latest success with me. They, too, have somehow been touched by what I do and how I do it, and they often tell me that they were inspired to accomplish something on their own because they saw what I had done.

The responses I have received throughout the years certainly have been gratifying and fulfilling. But it wasn't until my cousin Pat Perry first suggested there was a book in me, and until West Hollywood PR diva Helen Goss truly lit a fire under my butt, that I began to think of sharing my whole story. And I want to make it clear from the start that I am where I am today because of numerous people, events, and circumstances that have shaped my life, my way of thinking, and my reason for doing the things I do. I've just felt all along I was doing what I had to do—what was in me. I didn't have any choice. So now, taking Pat's idea and Helen's prodding, many blessings from above, and a sincere desire to give something back, I'm trying to do a little more. With this book, it is my intent to provide a detailed look at how *anyone,* even me, a relatively shy, introspective woman from Mount Vernon, New York, can excel in business and in life. I'll explain what I do, how I do it, and why I do it, and I'll show you what the fantastic results can be. I'll tell you how others do it, also, and you'll learn how these successful people got to where they are. And all of these methods, thoughts, and ideas will be illustrated by proven and real examples and experiences—my own and those of others.

I'll say right now that you may find a lot of my advice a bit "corny" or "hokey." But that's okay. I know it works, and if you try it, you'll see that for yourself. And I'll also say that we must all *strive* to do things I talk about—I really don't think anyone could do all of the things all of the time. *The fact of the matter is, most people don't do these things.* So when you do, you stand out. It helps make the world a better place.

Now I'll admit that sharing my "trade secrets" is a bit scary. After all, now you'll know (almost) *everything* about me. But I'm proud to be able to give something back. And . . .

I'm tellin' you—this shit works!

Before we get down to it, let me tell you how it all started for me.

Section One

In the Beginning

Chapter 1

The Beginning of The TWA

*T*he power is in every one of us to do anything we want. What separates the men from the boys, the women from the girls, those who make it and those who don't, the ordinary from the extraordinary, is perseverance—staying in the race. There are *no* excuses (race, sex, the economy) for not being able to do what you want to do. Sure, there are obstacles—but they're for somebody else to stumble on or over. Not for me—I pride myself on turning obstacles into stepping-stones. And not for you.

I found out about obstacles when, after finishing college and grad school and taking a job that was a natural extension of my training and education, I realized that this was *not* the profession I really, truly wanted.

That's right. With all those years—and all that tuition—under the bridge, with an undergraduate degree in psychology and sociology and a master's of science degree in social work, I found I was on the "wrong" path for me.

I'd never studied public relations, marketing, or communications. So how *did* I get into public relations?

After earning my master's, I worked at New York Hospital, using my education to work with terminally ill and physically challenged patients. I was there for about two years, and during that time it became increasingly obvious that I simply couldn't handle the demands of the job. Why? Because I took it so personally. The frustration of not actually being able to alter people's conditions was incredibly depressing. That, coupled with the reality that we could not save everyone, was overwhelming. After that period at the hospital I simply burned out. I had also decided that I wanted to make as much money as I could in this lifetime—legally—and it just wasn't going to happen in social work. I knew it was time for a change. It was time to take a risk.

The trouble is, if you don't risk anything, you risk even more.

—Erica Jong,
American
writer

Sometime during what would be my last several months at the hospital, the buzz was going around the nurses' station that the great jazz legend Miles Davis was a patient on another floor. I had heard that Miles was not one of the friendliest people walking the planet. But I took a chance and decided to take my shy self up to meet a man I had long admired and revered as a musical artist.

You have to face your phobias. I took the risk and went up to introduce myself. It paid off. The first meeting wasn't earth-shattering—he was surprisingly "normal," and he took to me as if I were just an old friend. (And I would find out later that Miles was like that with a lot of people he met—he had a radar detector for whether you were "real" or not.) After several daily visits, Miles and I just clicked. We established that all-important rapport and kept in touch after he left the hospital.

After meeting Miles, my urge—the actual need—for a career change became even stronger and more apparent. I just knew that the hospital and social work weren't for me over the long haul. But what else could I do? Meeting a force like Miles was not an everyday occurrence. Nor was my summoning up the courage to introduce myself to someone as well known as Miles Davis. I didn't know exactly what or why, but even then I felt inside that meeting Miles would have some kind of impact on my life. I firmly believe that destiny plays a major part in our lives and that we are most definitely led to certain events, circumstances, and opportunities. And if we take advantage of those occasions, they can make a positive impact on our lives.

A short time after meeting Miles, I was relaxing one day and reading the *Amsterdam News,* one of the country's largest Black newspapers. I happened to notice a small article about a public relations course being given at the YWCA at Fifty-third Street and Lexington Avenue in New York City. It was one of those "things that make you go 'Hmmmmm,'" as Arsenio says. Since my training and experience focused on dealing with people, why not public relations? Or, as I call it in the next chapter—"people" relations. So I took the course. Then I enrolled in another course given by the Publicity Club of New York. The classes were a bit dull, I must say, and it wasn't until New York PR honcho Lee Canaan came one night as a guest speaker that I really caught the PR bug.

I was immensely impressed with how Lee presented himself and the business. He had a self-assuredness about him, and he made PR sound exciting and challenging—

the ideas and ways of packaging someone or something and introducing them to the public. I thought he was the coolest "White boy" I'd ever seen, and he got me excited about the PR industry.

I then started to do volunteer work for local radio station WWRL, where Bob Law (activist/entrepreneur and host of his own nationally syndicated radio talk show), one of my first "ins" to the industry and a long and respected friend, showed me all kinds of ropes and facilitated introductions to many people. All of this prepared me for leaving the hospital and becoming the program administrator for the fledgling Black Filmmaker Foundation, a newly founded organization supported by the Rockefeller Foundation and the New York State Council of the Arts. I made publicity a specific part of my responsibilities. Warrington Hudlin, who later would produce the wildly popular *House Party* movie and then *Boomerang*, which starred a guy named Eddie Murphy, co-founded the BFF. (And it was Warrington—twelve years after we first met—who gave the Agency our first shot at handling movie publicity. The Agency now has a full-fledged film publicity division.)

To build my base of contacts, I started to attend the "right" functions. I went to art and photography exhibits, poetry readings, and the like. I built my public relations portfolio by doing publicity work for the BFF and by volunteering my services to local nonprofit organizations and to friends who were jazz musicians and needed some press for their gigs. I tried to latch on to anything I could do—I needed to make my résumé, which was largely social work oriented, start to reflect some PR experience. I also had to prove myself time and again to those who didn't take me seriously. After all, I had no real public relations training and no journalism experience. I would, however, take their apprehension about me—all new obstacles—as vitamins. I figure, if it doesn't kill you, it'll only make you stronger. Initially, people's doubts would piss me off, but then I'd say to myself, Okay, you won't talk to or deal with me today. That's okay. One day, you're gonna *want* to, or need to. Count on it! So I worked at it and worked at it and—starting from what I had learned from those two PR courses—became pretty much a self-taught practitioner of public relations.

I eventually moved on to become executive director of the Black-Owned Communications Alliance (BOCA), the trade association of media owners whose objective was to increase the use of Black-owned media outlets by national advertisers. After that, Sid Small, president of the American Urban Radio Network (formerly the National Black Network), tapped me to be director of the World Institute of Black Communications, which founded the annual CEBA (Communications Excellence to Black Audiences) Awards, the advertising competition designed to honor those agencies and organizations that do an outstanding job of communicating their messages to the Black consumer.

Then I got the PR job of my life at Essence Communications, Inc., heading up their public relations department and becoming director of corporate communications and the youngest vice president in the history of the company.

Then I started my own business.

But wait a minute. It wasn't all *that* simple and quick, of course. Nothing that's worth anything ever is. When it was time to move forward, it was time to do a lot of thinking—a lot of mental preparation. Chris Vaughn, a good friend and the former New York bureau chief of *The Hollywood Reporter,* gave me the following inspirational quote attributed to the famed philosopher Goethe:

> Until one is committed . . . there is hesitancy—the chance to draw back. . . . The moment one definitely commits oneself, the Providence moves too. *All sorts*

> *of things occur* to help one that would never otherwise have occurred. A whole stream of events issues from the decision raising in one's favor all manner of unforeseen incidences and meetings that would have come his way. Whatever you can do or dream, you can. Begin it. Boldness has genius, power, and magic in it. (emphasis added)

Once I committed myself to moving into PR, all sorts of things certainly did start to occur for me. And each one of those positions I mentioned came about with the assistance of the many people who saw something in me and took a risk of their own by helping me out. I know that to get where I am today, it took more than my own talent and hard work. It took the help of people who believed in me—and in what I could do, given the chance. So many people provided me with an incredible assortment of opportunities—stepping-stones—which I never failed to take advantage of. In the middle of all that blur you read a minute ago, I also worked for a month at *Black Enterprise* magazine in the public relations department, then headed by a woman named Carolyn Odom. She noticed my drive, so she steered me over to Wayne Sobers, who was then executive vice president of Earl Graves Inc. and a core member of BOCA, where it so happened that my work was also being observed by one of the other members—Ed Lewis, co-founder of Essence Communications, Inc. I'll always give thanks that he, too, saw something in me! When I went over to WIBC to handle the CEBA awards, I was there just six months when Ed Lewis called and offered me employment at ECI. It was my dream job: the first opportunity to have a full-time, professional public relations position. But at the time we were right in the middle of coordinating the huge, annual CEBA dinner, and in all good conscience I did not feel I could leave that hanging. So I had to take another risk. Did I dare ask this man to consider waiting? Well, yes. I also offered my assistance in handling any of the company's interim needs. And wait he did, much to my surprise. For six months! So I was on my way to building the foundation that would lead to my opening the doors to The Terrie Williams Agency.

I started to construct my own network of "people to know." I maintained relationships with those for whom I did volunteer work. When I met someone new, I would make sure to follow up with a note or letter. I kept in touch with Miles Davis and all the people I met through my various jobs in the communications field.

My work at Essence Communications (publishers of the magazine and producers of the nationally syndicated television show) led to an ever-expanding contact list of celebrities, movers and shakers, politicians, and civic leaders. And I continued to work even harder at cultivating my relationships and building my reputation in the PR world by getting involved with numerous PR industry associations and organizations, including the New York chapter of the PRSA (Public Relations Society of America), for which I served a two-year stint as secretary and then treasurer.

> *Our destiny is largely in our own hands. . . . If we succeed in the race for life, it must be by our own energies and our own exertions.*
>
> —FREDERICK DOUGLASS

Then, destiny kicked in again. I say today that it was always in my blood to start my own PR firm. But I again give credit to the fates that brought me to what I was born to do. My work at Essence and my friendship with Miles brought me into circles of people I would only dream of meeting, let alone having dinner with. And it was at just such a dinner—a sixtieth birthday celebration for Miles given by his then wife, Cicely Tyson (who would also later encourage Miles to have me represent him), on a yacht in Marina del Rey, California—that I got the chance to meet Eddie Murphy.

Now, of course, I wasn't just going to walk up to Eddie and say, "Hey, Eddie, I'm thinking of starting a public relations firm. Why not be my first client?"

What I did do that night on the yacht, knowing it might not be appropriate to approach Eddie (you don't just walk up to a superstar), was to create a natural inroad to him. And that path was laid before me by the people who were there *with* Eddie. So I started talking with these guys, and they were very receptive and friendly. I developed a rapport with Kenneth Frith, one of Eddie's top aides and now a coordinating producer on Eddie's film and music projects, and Ray Murphy Jr., Eddie's cousin, who is now vice president of production at Eddie Murphy Productions.

After that night, and for the next two years, I sent them notes, letters, articles of interest—whatever it took to further establish and cement the relationship. It worked. Kenneth started to invite me to some of their parties, to see Eddie do his stand-up routine—even to the filming of the concert movie *Raw*. Over that period of time I heard—twice—that Eddie was looking for a personal publicist. That was a little unbelievable to me at the time—the man had been amazingly successful for a number of years and had never had a personal public relations person. Eddie was simply using the publicity machine at Paramount Studios, where he was under contract.

It was another thing that made me go "Hmmm . . ." But I didn't give it too much thought at the time, and I continued to go about my business at Essence—building up their public relations department, publicizing the company's activities, and giving my usual 110 percent. And I kept reaching out to people and building my contacts.

Along the way I came across the work of Richard Brown, who teaches the popular, long-running New School for Social Research film course. He counts among his close friends many of the top film actors and moviemakers. Richard had done a commentary for television's *Entertainment Tonight* that I had particularly liked, so I wrote him a note to tell him so. He responded to me, and we stayed in touch. He even started inviting me to be his guest at screenings he held. At one special screening, the Oscar-winning film *Moonstruck* was being shown for Platinum American Express card holders, and Richard invited me to stop by. Dwight Brown, former head of the New York Film Critics Circle, and I were the only people of color at the event. At one point during the evening this White woman, Marge Fink, came up to me in the restroom. She said she didn't know who I was, but she wanted to know why I was there. I'm thinking to myself, Who is this incredibly nosy White woman? (Don't worry, I know Marge won't take offense at that. She *is* nosy. And loud. And bold. And people tend to love her for it.) So Marge (a public relations consultant) and I struck up a conversation, and it turned out we did know one another from telephone contact. In the course of the conversation, she said to me, "And I heard Eddie Murphy's looking for a PR person. . . ."

That was the third time I had heard that. Third time's the charm, right? I just *knew* at that precise moment that I was supposed to represent Eddie Murphy, even though I didn't know how, when, or where.

So I said to myself, This is it; it's now or never. The next day I put together a package for Eddie—an overview of my duties and accomplishments at ECI and a list of some of the people who could vouch for my work and my character. By that time a number of other well-known individuals, politicians, and movers and shakers had come to know me and my "style." I also briefly outlined some things I could do for him and explained that I was thinking of opening my own public relations company.

That's really all I had to go on. But I sent it over to Eddie anyway—a copy to his house and his office. Bold? Most definitely! Who did I think I was? But you gotta take a risk to get anywhere in life.

I will never forget the night I called over to Eddie's home and was speaking with Ray. I was just calling to say hello, and before Ray and I had the opportunity to really start talking, he said, "Hold on a second, Terrie. Eddie's here and wants to talk to you."

I gotta tell you, when Eddie Murphy, the number one box office champion, one of the most recognizable stars in the world, got on the phone and said, "I got your package, and I would love to have you represent me," I cried. Those were his exact words. I'll never forget them.

For Eddie to have that kind of confidence in me made a tremendous statement. So I took it as a sign from God that I was supposed to launch my own business—even though I had no agency experience, no money, and didn't know how to run a company. I knew it was my calling. To be able to launch a business with the number one box office draw in the world . . . Check that out!

So launch my own business I did. The folks at Essence were generous—they actually gave me their blessing—to let me begin while still there. The support given to me by Ed Lewis, editor in chief Susan Taylor, President Clarence Smith, and Elaine Williams, VP of human resources, as I began to make the transition from vice president of their company to founder and president of my own firm, was more than I could have asked for. They consistently nurture the entrepreneurial spirit in women—as they did with me and many others—and for their guidance and backing I will be forever grateful.

My last few months at Essence were spent orienting my successor, saving money, looking for office space and equipment, and saving money. And saving money.

You'd think that with all that saving, there would have been a lot of money. Think again. But then good luck entered the picture once again. I learned that another PR practitioner, David Fenton, was moving his operation to Washington, D.C., and needed to be in New York only once a month, so he was looking for someone to sublease his large office space for the nine months left on his lease. That was it! We made a deal. It was truly unbelievable how everything fell into place. There was enough room for me and my start-up staff of two, including Joe Cooney, my coauthor, who left his position as publicity coordinator at Essence to join me. My friend Leah Wilcox gave me a couple of chairs (including my "executive" desk chair, which we still use today), but the rest of the furniture was already there, as was the office equipment, phones, everything! All I really needed were a few odds and ends (purchased with my savings) and some starting capital (the rest of my savings). And so the first offices of The Terrie Williams Agency opened for business at 250 W. 57th Street in Manhattan, the Fisk Building, which houses a number of hot entertainment-related businesses. And we had Eddie Murphy as our first client, with Miles Davis signing on shortly thereafter.

Not bad, huh?

Chapter 2

The Beginning of TW

*W*hat you have just read could not have been accomplished if I hadn't had a solid foundation of life's lessons upon which to build my success. I am certainly aware of the countless stories of accomplishment by people who have had little or nothing to build on. And to those achievers who found a way to build their own road to success, my sincere commendations and respect. But I know that in my case I was fortunate enough to have the support of an encouraging family and the opportunity for a good education. Yet I still had to overcome obstacles—everyone does. I'd like to share a little of my personal background with you to give you an idea of just who I am and how I got here.

We've all heard the glamorous movie starlet, the mega-successful businessperson, or one of the so-called supermodels say something like "I was always the 'ugly duckling' in high school" or "I really was a geek when I was a teenager."

I can relate, in a way. In my case, I always felt "average" when I was growing up, even though my parents always instilled in me a desire to excel. Speaking of my parents, I gotta tell you that I'm the product of some pretty good stock. My mom, Marie, is one of the strongest and most inspiring women I know. One of nine children born to a sharecropper, she is the only one in her family to complete high school and then go on to college and graduate school (after my sister and I had finished our schooling). My grandmother was left by her husband and had to raise my mother and her eight siblings alone.

My father, Charles, is a self-taught man, forced to leave school at an early age to help his mother, who also had been left by her husband, support her five children. Consequently he was only able to finish the eleventh grade, yet he educated himself through military service and from books and encyclopedias. He showed me long ago the importance of "finding a way" to do what you want, and need, to do. When the trucking company he worked for closed down, leaving him without work, I remember my little girl imagination conjuring up all sorts of horrors: that we would starve (actually perish!) if my dad didn't have a job. But he managed to locate a partner who was willing and able to join forces, and he started his own trucking business.

I know that my parents wanted the best that was possible for me and my sister, Lani, especially because their own childhood years were difficult. So I attended good schools—even nursery school at the YMHA and YWHA (Young Men and Young Women's Hebrew Association, which was a bit of a distinction—you won't find too many little Black kids at a Jewish nursery school). I was one of the first students to participate in the city's open enrollment program and transferred from the Robert Fulton School on the predominately Black south side of Mount Vernon where I lived to the north side predominantly White Pennington school, which offered a more solid education because they had better resources and facilities. And while most kids were bused, my parents and a friend carpooled us to school.

I was always the recipient of the ever-present encouragement from my parents. Yet, as I said, as a young student I always considered myself nothing more than "average." In fact, you know how they have the different reading or learning "levels" in school? Well, I could count on being right in the middle. Little miss mediocre. In addition, everyone regarded me as the typical "Miss Goody Two-shoes." My mother even recalls the occasions when I invited my teachers home for lunch. A bit of a geek, a dweeb, a nerdette? You betcha!

Again, we hear all the time that the successful/beautiful/happening people of today were nerds, maybe a bit "homely" and "not with it" when they were younger. I felt the same way when I was younger and could certainly empathize with Oprah Winfrey, who recalls that she hated the thick, black-rimmed glasses she wore as a high school student. Or Mercedes Ruehl, the Oscar Award–winning actress, who has said that she was always a timid person—scared of everything; in fact, she even eluded success because she was afraid she didn't have the right stuff to handle it. And supermodel Paulina Porsikova, who remembers that her classmates in high school considered her an outcast and even beat her up! Even Harrison Ford, that machoest of macho Indiana Jones, says he used to be a favorite target of the schoolyard bullies. "I was a real class wimp," says one of the world's most famous tough-guy actors. Or let me introduce you to John Sculley, former chairman and CEO of Apple computers. At a time when most personal computer manufacturers—even the seemingly invincible giant IBM—were struggling, Apple could boast record-setting revenues of more than $7 billion (that's with a *b*) for 1992. Sculley, the energetic and visionary company leader, grew up in New York City and was, by his own admission, a nerd. He was hindered by a severe speech impediment, and he lived mainly in the interior world of his own imagination until his mid-teens, when, with the help of a hypnotist, he overcame his stammering. "I couldn't even walk into a store and buy a pack of gum," said the man who is now one of the corporate world's most sought-after speakers.

So today, when I speak at colleges and universities or for business groups, I always say: "If you're feeling a little bit weird, or out of place, not to worry. It means you are destined for great things!" No amount of not fitting in will stand in the way of your path to success if you don't let it. For sure, there isn't *one* person of all the "cool" people back at Nichols Junior High or at Mount Vernon High School I'd want to change places with today. Not one.

Probably we all felt a bit "out of it" at one time or another when we were growing up. But you'll notice that all those mentioned earlier are surely accomplished now. And that's because there is another similarity successful people share—the burning desire to become the best at what they do. Whether it was the result of an outside influence—a mentor or role model—or simply an inner strength that suddenly blossomed, all those successful folks realized at some point that it was time for a change.

For me it began in my high school years, when the desire to distinguish myself from others—the yearning to be something special—became something of an obsession. Thus began my personal quest to find a way to make a difference. I started to find that edge that would enable me to stand out. I must also point out that my parents had also instilled in me a great respect for other human beings, and I knew this would eventually lead me into a field that would involve helping people on a personal level. I remember that for several years my family went to the St. Agatha Home—a refuge for disadvantaged and orphaned children—in Nanuet, New York (a small town not too far from Mount Vernon), and we'd bring a little girl from an impoverished family home with us on weekends. You can just imagine what that meant for that girl. Her joy made me realize that I wanted to—as much as possible—find a way to make a difference in people's lives.

I always kept that in my mind, and after graduating from high school, I entered Brandeis University in Waltham, Massachusetts. I was majoring in psychology and sociology, figuring that if I was going to help people, I should know what makes them tick. Right? Right.

What I didn't count on, however, was the statistics course that was a prerequisite for the five-year doctoral program in clinical psychology I was planning to get into. Stats kicked my ass—twice. I just couldn't handle it. So I did some research and found that social work (a two-year program!) was a viable alternative. I could still "save the world" but didn't have to master statistics.

Bingo. I "found a way," as my father had showed me.

And let me stress a thing or two about what it meant—and took—for a Black woman from Mount Vernon, New York, to attend Brandeis University, a prestigious Jewish institution of higher learning in Massachusetts. Bottom line: I had to prove myself—to others and, most important, to me. Marketing yourself is one of the most important ways to get ahead in this world, whether it be in college, at work, or in your personal life. And I knew that nobody would notice me (the "average" girl) unless I did something about it. I had to do public relations for *me*.

Sure it was challenging to gain entry to a school like Brandeis. Yes, my grades were good enough, and the SAT scores were okay. But what set me apart, what got me accepted, were all the "extras" that came with my application. I was a standout in extracurricular activities. You name it, I did it: community-related events; clubs; school societies. I was president of my sophomore class and also president of the Keyette Club, a distinguished civic service organization at the school. I was even selected by my high school to be one of two students to participate in a student exchange program—I got to spend the summer in Cali, Colombia (South America). (I must give credit and thanks to my high school division principal, Morris Warren, a man who dedicated his life to seeing—and nurturing—the potential in students. He helped guide me throughout my high school years, got me into a college prep course that enabled me to leave high school a year early, and even facilitated my admission to Brandeis.)

Finally graduation day came at Brandeis, and a BA was bestowed upon me—cum laude, mind you. And then it was on to Columbia University in New York, where I earned my master's. Then it was on to the job at New York Hospital, working with terminally ill patients. And I must pay my deepest respect and admiration to all those nurses, social workers, and doctors out there who have the caring, understanding, and pure guts to stick with their careers. Those professions, along with teaching—the shaping of young people's minds—are among the most noble of undertakings. Such people are indeed living saints. But that world burned me out.

And then I met Miles Davis. (I deeply miss Miles. The world lost a legend a couple of years ago. I lost a friend.)

Then a few years later, there I was—starting my own company, in a totally different career from the one for which I had studied and trained. Was I ready? And more important, was there full commitment there? I remember that I had left New York Hospital on a Friday, to start at the Black Filmmaker Foundation on Monday. The BFF was a new nonprofit organization—read: A regular paycheck might be iffy at best. Hell, they didn't even have an office at first—I worked out of my apartment for three months. Was I crazy? I would be giving up all my free doctor visits and all my unemployment benefits, and I'd have to pay for my own health insurance! I must thank my mom once again for being there. I remember her offering any help she might be able to provide and, above all, saying to me, "If that's what you really want to do, go for it. I'm here."

Always remember that whatever you do, whatever your plans and goals, you must honestly look into yourself and know that you will give all that it takes to reach your objectives. You don't get anything in life without taking a chance. I was on my way, knowing that it was a risk. But I also knew:

> *Far better it is to try glorious things, even though checkered with failures, than to be ranked with those poor souls who neither enjoy much, nor suffer much. For they live in that gray twilight that knows not victory or defeat.*
>
> —Teddy Roosevelt

Section Two

Relationships

Chapter 3

Be a People Person

I have always found that the most important thing to remember in business, in school—*in life*—is this: We're all just people! It doesn't matter what kind of face you put before the public. Forget about "judging a book by its cover." Deep down we are all fragile human beings, each one of us a mixture of pain, joy, suffering, hopes, victories, and defeats.

Once you realize this, you can begin successfully to relate to others—by treating everyone the same, by thinking about the person you're dealing with, and by doing "that little extra." By being a people person, your level of success and your *life* will improve.

Renowned poet Maya Angelou, who spoke at President Clinton's inauguration, has for many years stirred us with her words. Her writing reaches our souls and makes us believe in our world and ourselves—as people. Just prior to the 1993 inauguration, Ms. Angelou was asked by the

Los Angeles Times about America's commonalities. She responded:

> Everybody in the world wants the same thing. Everybody. Everybody in the world—the president of the bank and the drug addict—everybody at some point in his/her most private place wants the same thing. Everybody wants to be needed. Everybody would like a job that he/she can do well and for which there would be respectable compensation. Everybody wants to love somebody . . . everybody wants safe streets, safe homes, good food to eat. . . . Everybody. There's no mystery.

Dealing with people is an everyday occurrence, taking up most of our waking moments. And while we all need some solitude now and then, our interactions with others are probably the most important parts of our lives. How we interact with our fellow human beings does more to shape our lives, our reputations, and our careers than any other single thing we do. It is imperative to understand that underneath the image we project, we are identical. We are human beings. And, again, we are here on the planet to hold each other up and to support one another. The challenges of life far outweigh the joys—and that's why we need to be there for each other.

One thing I've absorbed working with, hanging out with, and dealing with well-known personalities is that they too are really just people. And I've crossed paths with some incredibly genuine, real human beings who just happen to be "stars"—Nancy Wilson, Ann Jillian, Hammer, Gregory Hines, Cissy Houston, Danny Aiello, Halle Berry, Patti LaBelle. We're all human—and you will garner respect if you treat everyone as if they were the next-door neighbor. Look them in the eye, treat them as equals, and you will earn that person's respect. Most celebrities—pretty much like everybody—aren't looking for you to kiss their ass. Most people do just that—kiss ass and "yes" them to death. (Some personalities, of course, thrive on it: the musical artist who wouldn't get into a limo because it was "the wrong color"; the actor who gave a flight attendant a dollar to go get him a paper just before takeoff. If he was really all that, why didn't he have an assistant that traveled with him?)

But when you act with honesty and straightforwardness, it is appreciated and admired, not only by well-known people, but by everyone. Underneath it all, we're all the same.

Michael Bivins hit fame and fortune as one of the co-founders and young stars of the hit group New Edition. The multi-award-winning star then went on to form the group BBD (Bell, Biv, Devoe), he discovered the platinum-selling groups Boyz II Men and Another Bad Creation, and he is now president of Biv 10 Records. He is one of the country's leading young entrepreneurs, and although Bivins could have let all that fame go to his head he remains an honest, open person who credits his success to his family support. He is keenly aware of those who helped him get where he is. He is a real people person.

When speaking to a crowd at industry-related seminars, or when I'm on a panel addressing a group of students or young professionals, I often paraphrase a man who truly inspired me: Henry Rogers, co-founder of the entertainment public relations giant Rogers and Cowan and one of the most successful public relations pros of our time. In his book, *Rogers' Rules for Success,* Roger stated what I believe to be the ultimate rule of thumb. To me, this is literally the Eleventh Commandment—a philosophy that should be part of our professional and personal lives. In part, Rogers says:

> Understand that your relationship with people (whether inherited or acquired, conscious or unconscious) has as much to do with your success as all your professional knowledge—maybe even more. Believe it. The ability to relate favorably to people may hit you as something intangible, but the results are absolutely tangible. . . . It is that characteristic about your personality that wins love and respect. . . . And it enables your business associates to forgive your oversights, mistakes, and failures—those things that make us human.

Reread that one more time. Comprehend it, believe it, act upon it, share it with others. The world—*your* world—will be a better place because of it.

I am a people person. I've ascribed to that particular way of interacting with people, as have many successful people. You can, too! Why? Because it works.

To President Clinton's friends, his success is proof that there is indeed something special about the man—he moves people in an extraordinary fashion. Those who have known him for a long time have said that his gift for touching those he meets is "uncommon" and that it's at the center of what he's all about. Think about those photos you see of him all the time—at a McDonald's or a youth center. He gets *close* to people! During the summer of 1992 when the midwestern states were ravaged by floods, Mr. Clinton visited the citizens of Des Moines, Iowa, who were particularly hard hit. A woman in the crowd never expected to meet the president that day but in fact ended up crying in his arms. The picture of Clinton comforting this sobbing woman was printed in practically every paper in the country. A follow-up story in *People* magazine quoted the woman as saying, "He gave me a serious look when I walked up. The eye contact made me burst into tears." And in a diner in Queens, New York, as the chief of state was campaigning to sell his health care package, a woman broke down as she described how she could not get health care for her terminally ill son. Mr. Clinton comforted her (held her hand, in fact) and others with reassuring pats on the back and words of understanding.

President Clinton typifies the way of interacting I'm explaining here. I draw inspiration from many of his qualities. For instance, he has tunnel vision and is always totally focused. But the crucial component of his success is that even when faced with problems, he overcomes them by being an honest, real human being. Remember the Gennifer Flowers scandal? Clinton explained the situation by confronting it and, with his wife's assistance, convinced the public that their private life was just that—private—and would have no effect on the way he would run the country. The public was responsive, I believe, because they saw the human side of Clinton.

And I must point out that in the first few months of his presidency, Bill Clinton faced a number of challenges and made some decisions that had a negative impact on popularity. But regardless of how the history books will look at the Clinton years, the man will always be remembered and respected for his "people" relations. I remember seeing him one time on the cable station C-SPAN, which was covering a White House open house. It was truly awesome to watch Clinton, after being prepped by an adviser, meet and greet each person by their first name, with a warm smile and a comment. And while we all certainly can't live in the White House (and maybe we wouldn't want to be in such a spotlight—the "fish bowl" is a bitch), we can certainly learn from Mr. Clinton's ways and apply them to our own lives.

Mrs. Clinton—Hillary Rodham, that is—also is known to be a "down home" people person. She is known to care little enough about outer trappings that she could wait until the day before her wedding to buy her dress. When she and her husband occupied the governor's mansion, she reportedly used to run around Little Rock, Arkansas, in an old car, dressed in her everyday shorts and T-shirts. She cares about and is sensitive to those she meets. Hillary Rodham Clinton's life reflects what's happening in the lives of lots of women: she is deeply involved with her work, her causes, and her family. You also see her often in news photos or on television getting truly close to those she is dealing with.

Another really successful man who is also known to be a "people person" is Clint Eastwood, one of the most enduring and beloved actors of the last three decades. Clint has always been portrayed on the screen as the ultimate tough guy: "Go ahead . . . make my day" shot pangs of fear through everyone who watched him utter those words on the big screen. Yet in real life, Eastwood is famous for being a nice guy. He treats his friends, those who work on his movies, and everyone with whom he comes in contact with respect and dignity. He's cultivated a circle of friends and working colleagues who have stood by his side through the ups and downs of a Hollywood career. Eastwood, of course, has seen mostly "ups," because of his dedication to his work and his honesty and integrity. The film studios love him as an actor because his movies always make money; they love him as a producer and director because he makes quality movies—and brings his films in under budget. He does what he says he's going to do and has never had one of those infamous Hollywood egos.

When Eastwood copped a slew of Academy Awards in March of 1993, it was certainly because of his great work in *Unforgiven*. But it was also because—as the critics predicted beforehand—Eastwood was a sentimental favorite. Everyone, even the academy, likes him.

As I mentioned, my business offers me the opportunity to meet many famous people. As I've said a million times before, celebrities are no different from "regular" people. Some are quite nice and affable, even normal in spite of the ego-altering adulation that is synonymous with fame. Some, unfortunately (not *my* clients, of course), have let their stardom obliterate their need to be human.

Arthur Ashe, I'm proud to say, was a person I was privileged to know and work with. One of the most recognizable people in the world, this great man was a true celebrity in every sense. His accomplishments in the sport of tennis—made even more visible because he was the first Black "champion" in a White man's game—were legendary. Yet his huge popularity never touched him in a negative way. He was the truest "people person" I have ever met—he would talk to anyone, anytime. *And* he treated everyone as an equal. When he passed away, the sports world was saddened at the loss of one of their champions. Sportswriters eulogized the man who won Wimbledon, the man who broke many records and captured many titles. And they also wrote of a man who was a champion in all aspects of life. A reader of *The New York Times,* Paul A. Moses of Newport Beach, California, may have best captured the essence that was Arthur Ashe in his letter to the sports editor. Moses eloquently related the stories of the two times he'd met Ashe. The first was in 1972, when Moses was campaigning for George McGovern and was told that Arthur would speak at a reception of affluent supporters in New Jersey. On the day of the event, however, Arthur's agent confessed that he had not told Arthur of the scheduled engagement and that in fact Arthur was away on vacation but might be returning on a flight later that afternoon.

Moses rushed out to the airport and managed to get a note to Arthur via a friendly flight attendant. I'll let Moses tell the rest:

> At the time, Ashe was at the top of the tennis world, yet he was as unassuming and friendly as anyone I had ever met. He had no idea that he had been promised as a speaker, but there was no hint of irritation. . . . Ashe was the only Black at the reception, and he certainly had little time to prepare, but he moved easily and comfortably around the room . . . speaking eloquently on all the issues we discussed (in the car on the way to the event).
>
> Ten years later, I saw Ashe again at a reception. . . . I managed to get his attention for a moment and asked if he remembered our meeting. He did and asked how I had been, then paused and, with that characteristic ironic half smile of his, said, "We didn't do too well, did we?" and was gone into the crowd.
>
> McGovern may not have done well, but Arthur Ashe did splendidly. Ashe had nothing to gain personally, twenty years ago, when he spent a half day with me. What mattered to him was standing by commitments and being part of the world outside of tennis.

Arthur Ashe died of AIDS, which he contracted from a blood transfusion years before his death. As you probably know, he was eventually forced to announce to the world that he was, indeed, suffering from this tragic disease. Of course, it was a great shock to the general public. But many friends—even sportswriters—had known for years that he had the illness yet didn't talk about it or report it. And when Arthur did reveal his sickness, there was a tremendous outpouring of sympathy that he was even forced to reveal his private side. People felt he should not have had to do that. Why?

Because when you are a righteous person, the "angels in the universe" *protect* you. And Arthur Ashe was a true gentleman, a kind and generous spirit who treated everyone with respect and kindness. He had earned the attention of some universal angels himself.

Therefore, the scribes and friends kept quiet because they knew it just wasn't right to impose on a person's personal life—especially a man like Arthur Ashe. When Arthur Ashe left this world, an incredible member of the human race was lost. I only hope that we can all act a little Arthur-like and try to replace a bit of the kindness, grace, and dignity that left us when he died.

Chapter 4

You Never Know . . .

*W*e've mentioned that all people are identical—that deep down we are human beings. I want to share with you some other things about people that you should always keep in mind. Our adult lives are pieced together by the structure of our childhood and all that we experience growing up. Those of us fortunate enough to have been brought up in a caring, loving environment can certainly be thankful. But there are many, many people out there—some you know, some you will meet—who have faced challenges and hardships since the day they were born.

You never know what kind of personal baggage someone else is carrying. Whatever it is you may be admiring or lusting after that someone else has or does, count on the fact that there's some part of themselves that they don't like. You may covet something of someone else's—maybe their hair, their looks, their possessions. But you must know that that same person is not perfect—none of us are.

And you must know that the person you're yearning to be like is no doubt yearning to be like someone else.

> *Judge not the brother! There are secrets in his heart that you might weep to see.*
>
> —EGBERT MARTIN

So when you meet someone new, always keep in mind that you never know what their background is or what they are personally dealing with at the moment. Be aware that those people with whom you have had long relationships are carrying around a lifetime of experiences—good and bad—that have shaped their persona and their outlook on life. I've always thought that it would go a long way toward better, stronger relationships with those we work with, report to, and so on, if we tried to get some type of picture of their earlier life. Know that there are some basic givens operating there. Sometimes people's defenses are very hard to crack, so think: What motivates that person? What are their greatest fears?

You never know . . . what might be going on in a person's head, and the truth will often surprise you.

I had always kept in touch with my kindergarten teacher, a wonderful woman named Vickie Klein who taught me at the Robert Fulton School. When I was at Columbia's graduate school she contacted me and told me that she was pursuing graduate studies in social work after all these years and wanted to attend Yeshiva University. Could I give her suggestions about filling out the applications and doing the essay? I thought that was great—and it proved again that no matter what your status or position, we're all still people. I mean, here was my teacher calling me for assistance. A while after she got into Yeshiva, we had dinner together and she told me she had cancer. A few years later when she passed away, I attended the funeral—I was the only Black person there—and was quite surprised to hear myself mentioned in the eulogy as being a source of encouragement to her.

You never know . . . how your actions may affect another person.

A grocery store check-out clerk once wrote to advice columnist Ann Landers to complain that she had seen people buy "luxury" food items—like birthday cakes and bags of shrimp—with their food stamps. The writer went on to say that she thought all those people on welfare who treated themselves to such nonnecessities were "lazy and wasteful." A few weeks later Landers's column was devoted entirely to people who had responded to the grocery clerk. One woman wrote: "I didn't buy a cake, but I did buy a big bag of shrimp with food stamps. So what? My husband had been working at a plant for fifteen years when it shut down. The shrimp casserole I made was for our wedding anniversary dinner and lasted three days. Perhaps the grocery clerk who criticized that woman would have a different view of life after walking a mile in my shoes."

And the real heartbreaker: "I'm the woman who bought the $17 cake and paid for it with food stamps. I thought the check-out woman in the store would burn a hole through me with her eyes. What she didn't know (and I would never tell her) is that the cake was for my little girl's birthday. It will be her last. She has bone cancer and will probably be gone within six to eight months."

You never know . . . what other people are dealing with.

I became friends a while ago with a woman who had a five-year-old girl. My friend felt guilty, I guess, because she and the father hadn't married and they shared custody—she had her daughter on weekends. So I guess to compensate, whenever the youngster would ask for anything—"Mommy, I want this, I want that!"—my friend would immediately jump to grant the kid's wishes.

And (this truly blows me away) the kid says she needs "quiet time." How many five-year-olds do you know who ask for quiet time? Even though I think this is a little strange, I say okay . . . but then I ask my friend, "Do you take your 'quiet time' when your daughter takes hers, or are there times when you let her know you need your 'QT,' and she has to leave you alone?" Just as you (and I) thought, she takes her "QT" when her daughter is taking hers. Do we see a spoiled, self-centered person being formed? I'm thinking to myself, In about fifteen or twenty years this kid is gonna be driving her mate nuts because she's so demanding or needs her "quiet time" at the expense of their relationship. And that person—poor thing—won't have a clue as to why. But I'll know. I saw this kid's life unfolding. I've seen what was shaping her actions and demeanor.

You never know . . . what driving forces were present during someone's childhood. (But I do know that some of my friends and staff members really wonder what the hell was driving me thirty-five years ago.)

Everyone has heard of the flamboyant politician, activist, and civil rights crusader who in earlier years was often seen sporting a sweatsuit with a medallion around his neck: the Reverend Al Sharpton. If you haven't, you're either living in a cave or have simply paid no attention to the world going on around you. Anyway, Reverend Al has quite a reputation. And I must admit that I was one of those people who—for a while—just took what I had heard and seen for granted: 1) the statement communicated by the popular photo (it ran in every newspaper around) of Sharpton under a hairdryer getting his weekly hairdo; and

2) the generally accepted view that he was a publicity-hungry media monger who would show up at the opening of an envelope in an effort to get his name/face in the press.

Then one day I heard him speak at a dinner for a regional conference of the National Association of Black Journalists. And what he said really struck me. It went something like this: It doesn't matter how many degrees you have on the wall, or how many letters follow your name, it's what you *do* for other people that counts. History will not be impressed with your degree. He even went on to condemn those who believe their brilliance alone is responsible for their success. In truth, it's how many lives they lit up . . . and how many lives they've lifted as they climbed. He challenged those in the audience to go back into their communities to make a difference.

There I was—just like a lot of other uninformed people—thinking that this guy was not totally serious. And then I find out that he's really got his shit together! He's exactly right; we can't forget why we're here—to hold each other up. To keep the chain going.

Now that I've gotten past my initial response to superficialities, I admire Reverend Sharpton because he's a thorn in the side of the system. He reminds people of their responsibilities. He tells folks: "If you're the sole Black person in x, y, or z company . . . don't forget where you came from or who you are."

You never know . . . what deeper thoughts and intentions lurk in someone's heart and mind until you really listen up.

Always remember, too, that whoever you may be speaking with, or whoever you casually bump into, may be somebody in a position to help—or hurt—you. Mary Quello, the wife of Jim Quello, former chairman of the

FCC, dutifully kept track of her monthly cable bills and made sure that each was paid before the first of the month. When traveling once, she was delayed for the first time in eight years in sending off a check to her cable company. She was immediately hit with a late charge by the cable system, which had also picked that month to begin assessing fees for the converter box the Quellos had had without charge for eight years.

This was too much for the feisty Mrs. Quello, who went to the local cable office to voice her protest. "Congress and the FCC aren't going to let you get away with this," she exclaimed. An employee told her there was nothing the FCC could do about it, asking, "Why don't you call the FCC and find out?"

"I don't have to call the FCC," she replied. "I've been married to the chairman for fifty-six years."

You never know . . . whom you might unknowingly cross paths with.

It's all about connecting with people on a personal level. I have found throughout my career that getting to know someone's personal thoughts and feelings—their problems and hopes—enables you to make better connections with them on a business level. A client we had been working with failed to show up at her company event one night. I eventually found out that there had been some family problems she'd had to deal with. I sent off a card with a copy of the psalm "Footprints" (which is reprinted at the end of this chapter). About a month went by before I heard from the woman, but when she did call she acknowledged that the note and the inspirational message helped her and her family get through some rough times—she and her daughter even read it together before her daughter went into surgery.

I know today that's a part of the reason she has stuck with my Agency during some challenging times with the account.

In truth, there are no rules written on the planet that can't be bent, broken, or undone if you establish the right rapport with people. People do things that are beyond normal expectations and policy for others they like. Check it out. Be a people person, be nice to someone, and see the results. I guarantee that the gestures will come back to you. And when I speak today I always mention that the ability to relate successfully with people "turns contacts into contracts."

"Footprints"

One night a man had a dream. He dreamed he was walking along the beach with the Lord. Across the sky flashed scenes from his life. For each scene he noticed two sets of footprints. One belonged to him and one belonged to the Lord.

When the last scene had flashed before him, he saw that many times along the way, there was only one set of footprints. He also noticed that this happened during the lowest and saddest times in his life. "Lord, I noticed that during the troublesome times of my life there was only one set of footprints. I don't understand. When I needed you most, you left me."

The Lord replied, "My child. When you see only one set of footprints, it was then that I carried you."

—Anonymous

Chapter 5

What Goes Around, Comes Around

*T*hat old saying "What goes around, comes around" is no joke. Honestly, that's what keeps me from being evil sometimes—I'll think twice sometimes because I know it's gonna come back to me. And it's what keeps me going in challenging situations with people. Know that what you do and say will come back in some shape or form. It's the law of nature. And I'm tellin' you—payback is a bitch. A few quick examples:

Say you're driving to an important presentation, a new business meeting, or even a job interview. Somebody cuts you off, and you react—as most people would—by blowing your horn and yelling nasty things about their mother. Lo and behold, who's sitting before you at the presentation, or behind the desk at the job interview, but the very same person you wanted to strangle earlier.

Once, during my early years at Essence, I placed a call to a woman I was friendly with who worked at another magazine in their sales department. We knew a lot of the same people. The reason for my call was simply to request a copy of her media sales kit. Yet this woman flatly refused to help me out, for no good reason. It wasn't as if I were asking for top-secret files or anything. Honestly, it hurt my feelings—but life goes on. I never did get the package, and that always stuck in my mind. Wouldn't you know, four years later "Miss Thing" has the nerve to call me for a favor. Turns out she was interviewing for a job with the president of Essence, Clarence Smith, and she was looking for advice and information on how best to deal with him.

So, what do you think I did? What would you have done? Well, I didn't hold a grudge and just hang up on her. I did the right thing and answered her questions, prepared a package for her, and made sure she had gotten all that she requested. And you just know that wasn't the end of it . . . I had to use the opportunity to remind her of the importance of being there for one another. So I told her: "I would be remiss if I didn't remind you that a few short years ago, I asked you for some information and you flatly refused my request—for no good or apparent reason. Please let this be a life's lesson . . . we've all got to be there for one another. . . ."

Kathie Berlin is a studio executive and producer. Kathie is a major player in the entertainment industry. And she's close to First Lady Hillary Rodham Clinton and is heavily involved in the Hollywood political scene. A colleague of Kathie's once earned a prestigious position with the Democratic National Committee and, presuming she could continue to count on Kathie's assistance on a certain matter, called her for help. But Kathie learned that this woman had, on many occasions, acted disrespectfully toward her executive assistant at the time, Caroline Kim (actually looked right through her, know what I mean?). Kathie immediately advised the woman of this. Although the woman sent flowers to Caroline (a shallow attempt to appease Kathie, which was apparent), her relationship with Kathie was tarnished. Again, what goes around . . .

I like the fact that Kathie simply will not compromise her loyalty to her assistants. If someone treated Caroline wrong, and Kathie found out about it, she'd ask for an apology. I, too, cannot and will not tolerate anyone "dissing" my assistant or one on my team. It is totally uncalled for and is an action I find repulsive. Not only is it wrong, it doesn't make good business sense—we've had many "assistants" refer business our way. The thing to do is call someone on their behavior. When somebody does something wrong or disrespectful, you have to speak on it right away. If you don't say anything, the person may not even know they've crossed the good behavior line. And since we're all trying to be people persons, you need to connect with that person on a human level by advising them of their actions. If you don't, you're doing them a disservice.

It's all about one of my main points to live by: Treat people righteously. Or . . .

A few years back the actress Kim Basinger had a great deal going for her and was, in the eyes of many, the ultimate success story: incredible looks, a fabulous movie career, *star*dom—what millions of people dream of. But this blond bombshell reportedly had a bit of a problem dealing with people. There were stories that she was extremely difficult on the set of her movies—making unreal demands, throwing screaming fits. Then, back in March of 1993 Basinger made headlines when she was ordered by a jury to pay almost $9 million to an independent film producer because she had backed out of the movie *Boxing Helena*. Kim Masters, correspondent for *The Washington Post,* wrote of the judgment: "Everyone feels a certain delight when bad things happen to bad people. And if you took a poll in Hollywood, Kim Basinger would be high on the list of people who generate the very least amount of sympathy in times of distress. Many in Tinseltown were, in fact, happy to see Basinger get bashed." Masters quoted one studio executive as saying, "[Basinger] is so hated, it's unbelievable. 'Happy' is a nice cheap euphemism. People threw parties. Champagne sales were up."

Okay, so maybe Kim was having a year-long "bad hair day" or something. And sure, it's easy for us to join the crowd and hit someone who's down. But before you jump on the bashing bandwagon, stop to think that maybe Kim (or whoever it may be) was dealing with some personal hardships that we may never know about. Perhaps that is why she (or they) act a particular way. You should always keep an open mind as to what you *hear* about people—because it is not your own personal experience with them.

Remember, the point is that what you throw out into the universe comes back to you—one hundred times. Good *and* bad. And if you've been wronged by someone, you can do one of two things. You can be bitter about it and contemplate what would be a good revenge. Or you can remember this passage from the Bible's book of Corinthians: "Anyone whom you forgive, I also forgive." Break the negativity chain and respond, even to bad, with good. After all, you know it's coming back at you—so spare someone else the natural returns of "bad energy." Know that even if someone has done something against you, it is possible to forgive. Realize that you cannot judge others, for you do not know the circumstances or events that led to their actions—there's *always* another side. Look to the Creator for wisdom. You can't go wrong there.

If you still have doubts about what goes around . . . consider the following story. A widower by the name of Bill Cruxton lived in a small town called Chagrin Falls, Ohio. He was a lonely man who—since his wife's death—frequented the local diner, eating lunch and dinner there every day. The employees and customers became his family. One part-time waitress, seventeen-year-old Cara Wood, took a special interest in the old man. Her dad had passed away, and some felt that Cruxton acted as a father figure. If the old guy was ever late for a meal, Cara would call to make sure he was okay. When the teenager had to quit working because of conflicts with her school schedule, she still kept in contact with Cruxton, running errands for him and helping him around the house.

When Cruxton died at the age of eighty-two, he left $500,000 to a high school senior who had taken the time to give of herself. Her actions obviously made a real impact on him. Talk about the good that comes back!

What keeps me going through challenging situations with people is knowing that what they do *will* come back. I hope I will be around to see it. Maybe not—but I can rest easy, knowing it's coming back sooner or later.

Chapter 6

R-E-S-P-E-C-T

*I*n 1989 I was honored to be among those featured in an *Adweek* magazine special edition: "Women 1989 . . . Women's Survey." The writer—Casey Davidson—caught the essence of my being when she hung out in my office for a day. She noted in her article: "On the walls are signed photos from famous people. Repairmen wander in, and Williams talks to them in the same way she talks to [actor] Avery Brooks and to Miles Davis."

That's it! She captured the whole message—treat everyone the same, with respect and courtesy. Know that *no* one should be put on a pedestal, idollike. We have a tendency to forget that. Take from the best—learn from it, shape it, and adapt it to your own way of doing things. But don't idolize it. Everyone is a person first and a success second. You must also remember to treat *everyone* with the same kind of respect you expect from others. And if you treat everyone with respect, you'll never have to worry about the "bad" side of what goes around, comes around. Know what I'm saying?

Remember the extraordinary Hector Elizondo as the concierge in *Pretty Woman*? His character treated Julia Roberts—a "prostitute"—with respect and dignity. It wasn't because he was sucking up to the very wealthy Richard Gere character. He was treating another human being with respect.

Remember that a person's position in life should have absolutely nothing to do with how you interact with them. The janitor in the building is just as important—on the human being scale—as the CEO of the company. (Check this out: If the truth be told, the custodial staff could even tip you off to some inside info—they usually have knowledge about the goings-on in the company.) And you never know who will be in a position to help you.

A person's position in life should have absolutely nothing to do with how you interact with them. Treat everyone the same—from the superstar client to the student intern. Take Mike Ovitz, founder and chairman of Creative Artists Agency (CAA), who is widely regarded as the most powerful man in Hollywood. Yet this ultimate mogul, the man who has made deals involving billions of dollars, the man who instills fear in the hearts and minds (not to *me,* of course) of major studio executives, is still known to come across as a "regular guy." His friends praise his loyalty and honesty. Writers who have done features on him have said that Ovitz is easy to be around and that he acts as if he'd like to just sit around and chat. Above all, he comes across as "real," even "warm."

Or consider Anna Perez, a very special person. She was the press secretary for former First Lady Barbara Bush—the first woman of color to hold that position—and is now chief spokesperson for CAA (and Mike Ovitz). Although she would shudder at the thought of this, it so happens that this "power" association rubs off onto Anna, turning her into one of the most powerful women in Hollywood. (With all due respect to Suzanne de Passe, Oprah Winfrey, Whoopi Goldberg, Roseanne Arnold, and Barbra Streisand, of course.) Yet Anna, impressive as she is, is a low-key kind of person, very understated. She could certainly throw her weight around and tell everyone she meets who she is and what she does. But she doesn't do that. The lesson: No matter what your title or whom you work for, the way you act toward others shouldn't change. Often because they are associated with power, people become egomaniacal assholes—you know someone just like that, I'm sure. I know lots of them. Anna isn't like that; she's real, everyday good people.

Treat everyone as a human being—no matter where you are or what you're doing. I often make a point—when dining out—to make eye contact and/or say hello to the busboys and other hired help. Many upscale restaurants and country clubs tell their staff to avoid "intruding" on the customer by looking at them, the assumption being that the customers most certainly won't make eye contact with the staff. But I think that's absurd. The busboy is just as much a human being as the owner, and I treat him accordingly when I go out to dinner.

Remember the story of Lawrence Otis Graham, an African-American lawyer who went undercover as a busboy at a Connecticut country club. His experiences were the basis of a *New York* magazine cover story, in which he related what it was like to be an "invisible man." A film studio even bought the rights to do a movie on the guy. Here was a man—a successful attorney—who was immediately labeled inferior by his bosses, his co-workers, and the members of the club simply because he had hired on for the "menial" job of busboy. Club regulars treated him as if he weren't even there, talking freely of their prejudice and bigotry. The "N word" was commonly used, as were other derogatory racial terms and phrases. Women would even discuss the intimacies of their lives—who was cheating on whom, the affairs of their children. Little did they know that the lowly "busboy" was Harvard educated and highly successful—and it didn't seem to occur to them that he was listening to every word they said in his presence.

It is both sad and maddening to watch people's attitudes toward others change simply because of an assumption about status. As an example: It is a sure sign of personal respect for others to acknowledge when someone has earned a certain title. You address your physician as "Doctor," your college teacher as "Professor." Some lawyers like to be referred to as "Counselor." *But* if indeed you have earned a particular title, don't get all egoed out on people. It drives me crazy when someone automatically assumes superiority over someone else. I was reminded of this a while back when my assistant had placed a call to a colleague of mine who had received his Ph.D. She mistakenly addressed him as "Mr." and was promptly and sternly admonished that he was a "doctor" now, having completed his doctorate, and that he should be referred to as such. Well, excuse me! Congratulations on your achievement . . . well done! But don't make others feel inferior by throwing your (title) around. This guy made things even worse when I called him back and—on purpose—addressed him by his first name. He was immediately set to berate me with the "I'm a doctor" routine, but then he realized that it was I—an "equal" on his terms—who was calling. Then he lightened up. But I have to point out that there was no reason whatsoever for him to act differently with me and my assistant. We all deserve the courtesy of respect.

Another example of people's changing attitudes occurs on planes. It's unbelievably amazing how quickly a flight attendant's demeanor can be altered when he or she finds out your seat is in the front of the plane. I've actually witnessed a flight attendant get on the case of a colleague of mine because she was standing in the aisle talking to someone in the coach section. As soon as my friend informed the attendant that she was in business class and just visiting the person, Miss Thing says something like "Oh, I'm very sorry. No problem." That drives me nuts! And I know I personally have been treated in a slightly less than friendly manner when I'm flying coach. But when I'm in first or business class, it's a whole different story. Tell me, am I a different person because of where I sit? I don't think so.

And please, please, please, airline folks: There are people of color who can afford to fly first class or work for companies that foot the bill! Veronica Chambers, a successful author, former senior editor at *Premiere* magazine, who is now at *The New York Times Magazine,* just happens to wear dreadlocks, and told me she often gets grilled about whether or not she's in the right seat. And she'll be the only one asked. DeWayne Wickham, the celebrated syndicated columnist for *USA Today,* was also approached by a flight attendant as he was stowing his bags in the first-class cabin. She told him that there was plenty of room for his bags in coach, mistakenly assuming that he was flying economy instead of first class.

Helen Goss—who lit the fire in me to write this book—once told me of a conversation she had with her brother, Milton Stevenson. They were discussing how people earn—or lose—a sense of respect, and she and Milton shared a valuable lesson. Milton had said that he observed that Black people "acting White" get no respect because they will never be a better White person than a White person. Often, he said, one's ethnicity doesn't allow that person to move across the line . . . White people "acting

Black" doesn't work, either. The point: You must be loyal to yourself and to your people. That will earn you the proper respect.

Willie Williams, the police chief of Los Angeles—one of the nation's biggest examples of a city lacking in "people relations"—has brought a human touch (focusing on basic respect for people) to an incredibly tough assignment. His efforts have been widely praised.

"Willie Williams is the best thing that's happened to this city," said Bernard Kinsey, co-chairman of the Rebuild Los Angeles organization. "He's been getting his officers to work at treating the citizens as customers. They used to give immigrants fifty-two-dollar jaywalking tickets; that was a week's wages in some cases. He's now saying, 'Let's look at the human side of things, maybe just give a warning this first time, and make a friend of the guy.' "

For one more example of the results of treating everyone the same, think about the marriage of Elizabeth Taylor and Larry Fortensky. Here we have one of the world's richest and most glamorous and famous movie stars of all time, married to a construction worker. A regular guy. And how did this happen? What attracted these two "opposites"? I mean, their worlds were totally different. And the press had a field day with this, focusing an incredible amount of attention on why and how she'd been drawn to him. Nobody wondered what attracted him to her, as if she were automatically the "better" human being.

Well, first of all, love will do that to you. And yes, it probably happened because the two were undergoing drug and alcohol rehabilitation. It was a time when both were forced to bare their truest human qualities and frailties. And they connected at that time—on a purely human level, without the "star" trappings or misguided preconceptions. They respect each other—and are married to each other—as two human beings, not as a glamorous star and a blue-collar Joe.

There are lessons to be learned here. No matter what your position in the world, if you remember to treat others as fellow humans, you're a step ahead.

Chapter 7

You Never Get a Second Chance to Make a First Impression

*E*ven Liz and Larry had to have that first meeting, right? All relationships—fleeting or otherwise—start with an introduction. And as the saying goes, First impressions are everlasting. Therefore, how you introduce yourself—and others—and how you receive introductions are vitally important in establishing a good first impression. Once you have met someone new, remember that the person who was a stranger could now be a new friend, business acquaintance, even client. There are actually many different things to keep in mind when making an introduction, and I'll explain a few more in a minute. But first let me tell you about a friend of mine and the important lesson about introductions that he learned a long time ago.

When he was in high school, Doug Brown—who is now a successful entrepreneur—was attending a school function and had the chance to meet a football coach he really admired. Well, Doug offered a quick "How ya doin'," barely looked at the coach, and must have offered him a real wimp of a handclasp. The coach practically bellowed (as coaches tend to do), "Get back here and shake my hand like a man!" to an obviously embarrassed Doug. A firm handshake is very important. Nothing is worse (well, if pushed, I guess I could think of something) than one of those wet, clammy, limp, dishrag handshakes—you know the kind! That experience stuck with Doug for the rest of his life. In fact, later on that year, when he won a scholarship to a prestigious private school, he turned it down after meeting with the school's headmaster. Of course, everyone thought he had gone crazy, but he had a reason: The headmaster, Doug said, had a handshake that felt like a mound of Jell-O. As it turns out, the school Doug had turned down was eventually closed amid a scandal of wrongdoing by the institution's leaders—including the headmaster!

When you meet people, be mindful. Look them in the eye, be personable, and don't forget that firm handshake. And remember: Research studies show that people who smile are perceived to be more intelligent than those who don't.

When meeting someone, don't try to impress them because you just got your new, glossy cards with the important-sounding title printed below your name. It's not cool to go throwing your cards around. Remember to ask: "May I give you my card?" Conversely, don't just flat-out say to someone, "Can I have your card?" Instead, ask: "Is there a way to get in touch with you?" Or: "May I be in touch with you? What's the best way?" Don't push yourself on people or impose on their space. I even know people who don't have or carry cards on purpose—they don't want to be inundated. Taking it a step further, a well-known entrepreneur doesn't list his production company in the phonebook. He figures that if you want to be in touch with him, and if you're legitimate, you'll know how to reach him. Now, I wouldn't recommend that approach to everyone, but do be aware of being too pushy. It could ruin that all-important first impression.

Other introduction/make-the-right-impression tips include the following:

When introducing your spouse, if you say "This is my husband, Bob"—put the description before the name—it could be construed as demeaning to your husband or wife, implying that they belong to you, that the most important thing about them is that they are married to you. Try this: "This is Mary, my wife."

In the business world, introductions tend to be based on power and authority or rank. The rule: People of "lesser" authority are introduced to people of greater authority. Example: Mr./Ms. "higher-up," allow me to introduce Mr./Ms. "lesser authority."

And don't bring business right into the conversation when meeting someone by immediately asking "And what do you do?" It really gets me when people ask that right away, especially when it's asked to see if the person is worth their time, as though that by itself tells what kind of person they are. I'll even try to catch people off guard—my mother shared this with me—by quickly replying that I'm a prostitute or a drug dealer or something outrageous. Even when I went to my high school reunion I refrained from asking my former classmates "what they do." It can make people feel uncomfortable in that kind of situation. Remember, it doesn't make a difference. Try "What have you been up to?" That's always better.

For the folks out there who deal with the press: When introducing someone to a member of the media, make sure to mention that so-and-so is a working press person. This will communicate the message—especially to a celebrity, elected official, or corporate spokesperson—that the ensuing conversation may be "on the record."

If you find yourself in a group and do not know everyone, introduce yourself. Feeling slighted because you weren't introduced by another member of the group isn't productive, and remaining "unintroduced" puts you at a disadvantage. Don't hesitate—the longer you wait to say hello, the worse the situation gets. After a while, no one will care who you are. And how are you going to make a good impression if no one even knows who you are?

As a rule of thumb, always "rise to the occasion." Everyone—and this means women, too—should stand to greet new people entering the room or office. And when you're in an office, always rise and come around your desk to meet and greet visitors. I must admit that sometimes I just don't have the energy to come around my desk to greet someone. (I know you're probably thinking if I'm that tired, I should be at home in bed—and you're probably right.) I can get away with that when I find myself dragging by being honest with the person and saying something like "Please forgive me, I'm just kinda wiped out today." I stand up and offer my hand, but since I've been honest with the person, they'll understand why I'm stuck behind my desk. Keep in mind that a desk can be perceived as a "barrier." Try to make the person on the other side feel comfortable. If possible, sit on a couch or around a small table.

You should always think twice about just walking up to people who are in the public eye. Try to put yourself in the mind of that person—celebs are *always* approached by people requesting autographs, trying to pitch a movie idea or record project, or asking them to get involved in something. After a while everyone becomes a blur—and you are just another person, whizzing by as part of that blur. During my public speaking engagements, I always tell people that even though I'm "somewhat accomplished and known," I'm definitely mindful that 95 percent of the time it may not be cool just to confront a "VIP." I'm aware that I may be intruding on their space and privacy. So when I do see somebody really well known, someone I would like to meet, I may simply say "Hi, my name is Terrie Williams . . . just wanted to say I love your work" and then move on. Of course, if they respond to me, then the door is open. I take my cue from their body language—do they seem interested or distant? By now I've learned to "read" people's actions. What's best, though, is to have someone I *do* know (who also knows the celeb) do the introducing. That gives me a common bond with the person—the ideal beginning to a new relationship.

When approaching someone you've heard of or read about but may not know personally, remember that you do already know *something* about the person. This is your ticket. Introduce yourself, then say something like "I've read about you, and I'm very interested in your work/project." Then tell them why you're interested: "I'm working on something similar at the moment. . . ." You have just made the perfect connection—a personal one.

And don't *ever* forget: When you see someone you know at an event or in a restaurant, that person is bound to be with someone else, right? *Always, always* acknowledge that person first by making eye contact, nodding and saying hello, or quickly introducing yourself if appropriate. Then continue your conversation with your contact. "Sidekicks"—especially those who accompany well-known folks—are often ignored and disrespected, even treated as if they are invisible. Make a point to greet them and you will make a difference.

Speaking of restaurants, nothing will ruin a good first

impression faster than bad, sloppy table manners. Make sure your manners and table etiquette are up to speed. If not, take a course. And yes, I'm serious. Nothing could be more embarrassing at a business (or interview) lunch or dinner than realizing you don't know which fork to use.

You may have excellent business skills, but if you're out with the boss or a client and have table manners that would make a dog cringe, you're gonna be in trouble. You'll quickly find yourself in an awkward situation, having to fake it and hoping no one will notice (although they certainly will). So if you feel you lack the social graces, either take a course, read a manners book, or—as a last-ditch effort—follow the leads of others.

When the Agency was handling Dave Winfield, I was honored to attend a lunch hosted by former First Lady Barbara Bush at the home of the vice president. Dave was on the board of directors of Morehouse Medical College, and we joined about twenty-five other people for—as you can imagine—a very "proper" meal. The first course was waiting to be consumed by us, and I have to admit, I didn't know what the hell it was or what to do with it. I glanced around the table and—much to my relief—found quizzical looks on the faces of almost everyone. Finally someone broke the ice and asked aloud, "What *is* one supposed to do with this?" or something like that. Anyway, that broke everybody up and put us all at ease, and we then dug in. (We all ate it, but to this day I still don't know what it was.)

One more introduction tip: We have all been in the situation of meeting other people's parents. When you were a child, of course, it was always "Hello, Mr. so-and-so, Mrs. so-and-so." As adults, though, remember to provide assistance to the person you're introducing your family to by offering your parents' first *and* last names. This will avoid confusion for the person in the case(s) of a second marriage or divorce. I've often been on the other end, being told only "Terrie, this is my mother." I'll smile, say hi, and ask, "And does 'mother' have a name?"

Chapter 8

Teri, Terry, Terrie: What's in a Name?

*P*eople you meet will be flattered if you can call them by name after only a brief introduction. A few years back I found myself at a public relations industry luncheon, sitting at the same table with the megarich, megapowerful tycoon T. Boone Pickens, who was the day's guest speaker. We were introduced briefly, and I'm thinking, This guy is *too* large. . . . I don't even know why I'm in the same room with him. (I was still young and learning that we're all just people.) Well, later on in the afternoon T. Boone Pickens makes a point of mentioning me (*by name!*) and commenting on something I had said earlier. I was more than blown away, and that tremendously warm feeling of acceptance and recognition was one that will never leave me. I would have done anything for the guy—within reason, of course—just because of how he made me feel. Check it out sometime; you'll see exactly what I'm talking about. After that dinner, which was several years ago, I followed up with a letter to Mr. Pickens, and we corresponded for a while. He even sent me several autographed editorial cartoons in which he'd been the subject.

How did someone like Pickens remember "little old me"? Because he knows how to connect with people. And he knows how to remember the people he's just met. You, too, can acquire the knack for easy memorization. It's all based on the fact that your recall is best when you want to remember, when the words are simple, and when you reinforce them with repetition. Here's a brief lesson:

• Try to *be with* the individual at the moment you are meeting them—focus on them and who they are, what they are saying, and why you are talking to them.

• Set your priorities before you meet with a new group of people. Figure out whom you want to meet and why. This will motivate you and keep you interested in the people you meet.

• If you need to know only the person's first name—or last name—concentrate just on the part you need. (And keep in mind your "status" in certain situations—superiors in an office setting should initially be addressed as Mr. or Ms. Don't assume you're on a first-name basis right from the start. Let them offer you the option of calling them by their first names.) I still do this—just because you reach a certain "level" doesn't mean you can forgo the formalities. Even though we are all the same, people who may be older, or who have accomplished a great deal, should be accorded a certain amount of respect. And when people start addressing me as "Ms. Williams," I immediately try to make them feel more comfortable by telling them to call me just Terrie. It lets us connect better on the "we're all just people" level.

• As you meet each new person, say his or her name aloud. Repeat the name in your head several times and associate the person with his or her position: "Allison Davis, producer at the *Today* show."

I like to think I've pretty much mastered the art of remembering names because in my business I'm always bringing people together and introducing them—and it makes it a whole lot easier not to have to say, "May I have your name again?" But lots of times when you first meet someone, their name (and yours, also) goes in one ear and out the other—especially if you're in a room full of people. Here's a trick I use sometimes. If I get into a conversation with someone I've just met, I'll wait a few minutes and then suddenly blurt out, "So, what's my name?" This always surprises the person, who usually can't remember. Without skipping a beat, I laugh and then say, "That's okay, because I don't remember yours, either. How about we start all over again?" It always gets a chuckle and breaks the ice, and I guarantee the person will know my name from then on. And I'll know theirs, too.

Of course, there are bound to be times you will go totally blank and forget someone's name—and then have a need to introduce them to someone else. I meet hundreds of people each week, and it's nearly impossible to recall each person's name. Now, if you're with someone else and this happens to you, one solution is to say something like "Have you two met?" or "Do you two know each other?" and then immediately stoop down to pick up something you just "dropped," which will give them the chance to introduce themselves. But on most occasions it's best to be honest and straightforward about it. With a bit of tact, admit that you're suffering a "lapse," that you've "drawn a blank, forgive me." Stay away from the "I've forgotten your name . . . who *are* you?" approach. You run the risk of offending that person, who may feel you don't think they're worth remembering. And don't overapologize if you have misplaced someone's name—it just belabors the point.

If you are on the other side of the situation and someone seems to have (God forbid!) forgotten your name while making a round of introductions, jump right in there with a warm smile and your hand outstretched and offer your name. It will make everyone feel more comfortable.

Another hint: If you're with a gathering of a few people and don't recall everyone's name, and one more person joins the group, you can say, "Do you know so-and-so? Have the pleasure of introducing yourselves." And you're off the hook.

Also remember to get the correct pronunciation of people's names. To just presume that someone's name is pronounced a certain way—without checking and double checking—indicates a lack of interest (read: ignorance) on your part. And it can be quite embarrassing when you screw up. I'll never forget the time a television show booker called us because he thought we represented the songstress Sade. I felt sorry for the guy when he asked if "Sade" (he rhymed it with "blade") was available for an appearance on his show. And I felt even worse for him when, after I had politely corrected his pronunciation ("shah-day"), he replied, "Whatever." Not a good way to make an impression, know what I'm saying?

Misspelling a person's name can be equally embarrassing. I've often received correspondence that begins with Dear "Teri" or "Terri" or "Terry." There have even been a few addressed to *Mr.* Terrie Williams. This is an immediate turnoff—it shows that the writer didn't care enough to check out the spelling of my name or even my gender!

One of my first mentors, Ken Smikle, made up notecards for me that have the three wrong spellings of my name on the front with lines crossed through them. On the inside it says: "From T-E-R-R-I-E . . . Thanks." Great idea! I send it to people when they repeatedly spell my name wrong, and it never fails to get my point across.

Never assume. Do you remember that old adage about why you should never assume? Because it makes an *"a-s-s* out of *-u-* and *m-e.*" *Always* check the spelling and title of the person you are reaching out to. Remember the support staff—they can help you! If, when you're checking a spelling, someone says "I *think* it's . . ." watch out! Explain in a friendly, nonoffensive way that you must know for sure. Because if you still get the name wrong, the person you're writing to is not going to know you *tried* to get the correct info—they're just going to see the mistake. Check either directly with the person or the person's right hand.

Busy people who are inundated with papers, calls, and the like sometimes look for quick ways to "weed out" the volume—audio or visual "cues" that influence what will get seen first . . . and last. It's guaranteed that a document with a misspelled name or other error will end up at the bottom of the pile.

Also, don't ever believe that something as minor as a spelling error won't be noticed. Do you happen to recall when a former vice president of this country "corrected" a youngster's spelling and ended up "mashing" his reputation with one little potato-e? People *do* notice. The "*Mayflower* Madam" Sydney Biddle Barrows, the onetime prostitution ringleader whose ancestors came over on the *Mayflower,* once wrote a scathing letter to *The New York Times* blasting its editors for sloppiness. "Doubtless you'll think I'm taking this too seriously," she said, "but I've just had it with you people not spelling my name properly." Barrows said the newspaper constantly misspelled her first name as Sidney.

Even *Entertainment Weekly* magazine took the NBC network and Warner Bros. to task for this particular slip-up.

Seems an ad produced by NBC misspelled megadirector Steven Spielberg's name. And then Warner Bros. made a mistake in a press release that announced a film deal with *Jurassic Park* author Michael Crichton (they had it C*h*richton).

Chapter 9

The Art of Conversation

Of course, introductions generally lead to conversations. So, once you've met someone and have their name implanted firmly in your memory, you'll want to begin speaking with them. One surefire way to begin a discussion is to ask people something about themselves—what do they like to do for fun, what makes them laugh, and so on. People usually like this; just don't be too nosy. Showing a certain amount of interest in someone is flattering and will be remembered. And while you're engaged in conversation be mindful, and be an active listener.

That said—and let's be real—there are some boring people out there in this world. If you happen to come across one, just excuse yourself politely and move on. And again, be aware of subtle body language during a conversation—it's really annoying when you're talking with someone and you realize they're only partly with you. Their eyes are darting all over the place, and their head keeps bobbing around, pigeonlike, scoping out the crowd to see if someone "more important" is there. You wouldn't like to be faced with that, so remember—do unto others.

To avoid being labeled boring yourself, it helps to keep abreast of current events, popular culture, and other information relevant to those you are meeting. Remember to bring something more to the table than your appetite. In our office we skim through (the art of skimming will be explained in a minute) eight newspapers every morning and probably twenty to thirty periodicals, newsletters, and magazines a week. We even check out the society pages and see who's getting married. That all started because Ken Smikle instilled in me the importance of reading the papers every single day. Ken, who is an expert in Black consumer marketing, told me back when I was first starting out that I *had* to read *The New York Times* each morning. And I must admit that back then I battled against that and resisted like crazy, but I gotta give Ken his props—he helped me with my discipline, my writing, and my work habits by making sure I understood the advantages of simply reading newspapers and magazines. I now skim those eight papers a day and a whole slew of magazines and periodicals. Even when I travel, the first thing I do when I arrive in an airport is pick up that town's newspaper. You can pick up little tidbits or conversation starters by catching up on the local news and gossip. By the way, the art of "skimming" can be easily learned. If you're a news junkie (I am—and you should be, too!), you want to get as much news as possible, as quickly as possible, so that you'll always be on top of things. Learn to skim: first figure out what you're looking for when going through a publication and focus your attention on that specific area. Is it entertainment? sports? business? (To be a well-rounded individual, you should, of course, go through all the sections of a newspaper or magazine. But you can at least start out by concentrating on a specific area.) Next, scan the headlines of the stories—they will give you a quick idea as to whether or not you'll want to read the story. If indeed you are interested in a particular article, read just the first couple of paragraphs to get the important points and tear out the page so you can read the whole thing later. Also look for the names of people or businesses that interest you. The entertainment "gossip" columns help you here by putting the names of celebs in bold-face type. Go to the names first and read about the people of interest to you and your work. Bring your reading materials with you wherever you go. Catch up on your daily reading while traveling on the subway, waiting on line, or riding in a cab.

You want to know who's doing what with whom? who's writing about what? the latest trends? Read, read, read!

Keep a small-talk notebook and jot down notes of interest on various topics. If you're heading to a business dinner, take a look at that day's *Wall Street Journal* or business section of *The New York Times*, or *Black Enterprise*. Scan the first couple of paragraphs of the lead stories, fill up a few pages of your notebook, and study them before going to the dinner.

Read, read, read. If you're involved in the entertainment industry, you must be aware of the news coming out of Hollywood, New York, and other major entertainment centers. What are the latest stories running in *Variety, Ebony, The Hollywood Reporter?* How about *Vibe, Entertainment Weekly, People, US*?

Study the faces of key people so you'll know what they look like. Perhaps they'll be there at that next function. How can you approach them (appropriately, when the time's right, of course) and begin a conversation if you don't recognize them? It's very important to know who's who and who is doing what, and with whom, and where, and when and how.

Those who are well-rounded sources of information garner respect and admiration and can easily carry on a conversation with anyone else. This doesn't mean you have to be a genius, but it does require knowing what's going on around you. Besides, it's fun to know what's happening—the more you know, the more you can be a part of things and the more success you will find.

Remember, however, that knowing something is one thing; harping incessantly on one area of your knowledge is another thing altogether. Don't run the risk of repelling your audience by beating them over the head with useless facts, figures, and opinions. The only thing worse than not having a clue is being a boring windbag.

To initiate or "fire up" a conversation, you may want occasionally to be a little outrageous or daring. Perhaps you may begin a conversation on a controversial topic—carefully—or play devil's advocate in certain situations. But avoid being too one-sided or argumentative—you don't want to alienate people.

Even a simple statement can liven up your interactions. At the inaugural festivities in D.C. in 1993, Tony Wafford (creative director of my agency who lives in Los Angeles) and I noticed Dr. Ruth Westheimer walking out of the main event. Tony yelled out, "Hello, young lady!" after she had just passed us. Dr. Ruth stopped immediately, walked back to him (tickled pink), and chatted with him for a few minutes. Think he struck a chord?

Chapter 10

Maintaining Relationships

All the new people you have just been introduced to—and whose names you have remembered—are new contacts that can be developed into long-standing and mutually beneficial relationships. How you treat these contacts, and understanding that the relationship is reciprocal, is key. I gotta tell you, the importance of contacts cannot be stressed enough.

An article in *Reader's Digest* entitled "Little Things Do Mean a Lot," by Robert McGarvey, aptly illustrated my point. In fact, that title could have served well as the subtitle to this book. McGarvey writes of various people and how they got ahead by paying attention to the little things. McGarvey tells of a man named Harvey Mackay, who at age eighteen was told by his father about the importance of building a network of contacts. Heeding his father's advice, Mackay would write down the name and number of anyone he met whom he might want to get in touch with later. When Mackay was in his fifties and the owner of a successful envelope-making company in Minneapolis, he decided to write a book about the lessons he'd learned as a businessman.

A publisher agreed to take it on and set a run of only 10,000 copies. Mackay wanted a first printing of 100,000, so he pulled out his well-organized file of 6,500 names and addresses, many of them highly placed corporate executives and celebrities. With this starting list of potential buyers, Mackay was able to talk the publisher into a larger print run. *Swim with the Sharks Without Being Eaten Alive* became one of the best-selling business advice books of all time.

The importance of having the right contacts and knowing the right people is essential to what I'm saying here. It's how my career got off the ground and how you can make a difference in your own life. Let me relate a few more examples.

There's a guy in Las Vegas who is the son of a compulsive gambler. He has been investigated by the government for alleged ties to organized crime. He is hampered by an eye disease that may cause him to go blind. And this guy can't fill all the slots in a pair of gloves because he shot off his index finger a few years ago while handling a pistol in his office.

But Steve Wynn is also the owner of the spectacularly successful Mirage Resorts, Inc., which in 1992 claimed revenues of $833 million. This ambitious entrepreneur has scored one success after another, even though his first Las Vegas venture was a total flop. And it all started because Wynn, at the tender age of twenty-five, developed a friendship with one of the most powerful bankers in Las Vegas. By the age of thirty-one Wynn became the youngest casino chairman in the history of the city.

Or, there's a politician in Washington whom I mentioned before who has taken the art of making—and keeping—contacts and friends to a level beyond comparison. Throughout his life this gentleman, born of modest means, has stayed in touch with people through letters, phone calls, and notes. He has built an extraordinary network of loyalists—more than a few of whom occupy seats of major power and position—from scratch.

During his election campaign a couple of years ago, *The Wall Street Journal,* one of the most influential newspapers in the country, thought enough of this gentleman to profile him on its front page. The story, a glowing feature for the then candidate, reported that his reputation had been called into question in the face of allegations that he had dodged the draft. Immediately coming to his aid and defense were—among others—three old college buddies: an economist from Harvard, a Massachusetts state judge, and an editor at large from *Time* magazine.

Friends such as those three helped elect President Bill Clinton to the most powerful position in the world. Nobody collects friends like Clinton. And while the FOBs (Friends of Bill) will say they are drawn to him simply because of his charm and intelligence, the fact is Clinton attracts so many supporters because he works at it.

When I meet someone new, I make sure to follow up with a note or letter. Especially when starting out, or changing jobs or careers, you should keep a log of *everyone* you meet, come across, or even hear about. Send them notes and keep them updated on what you're doing. It's a surefire way to maintain relationships.

In the public relations/media business, some stories get into print or on the air because of relationships. I'm not minimizing the newsworthiness of the subject matter, but it's a fact that when you get down to it, relationships prevail. To illustrate the point, let me quote Ellin Sanger, one of half a dozen women featured in a *Cosmopolitan* magazine story about those who book talent for the various talk shows and news programs. The article explained all the different ways these bookers nab a top-notch star: persistence; having great contacts; bribery; being daring and bold—whatever it takes. But Sanger, who works for *20/20,* summed it all up. "You can have a great Rolodex and know the mechanics of booking," she said. "But that's not enough. In the end, it's all about relationships."

Always remember that relationships in any profession will impact heavily on your success or failure. Take the story of Marion Barry, former mayor of Washington, D.C., who was forced to leave office after his bout with drugs. Many powerful people have been toppled by hearsay, conjecture, rumors of wrongdoing. But Barry was literally caught in the act—and on videotape—of breaking the law. His political career was certainly destroyed when that tape was played. Or was it? A scant three years after he was convicted of the crime and served time in prison, Barry was back in the political arena as a D.C. council member, simply because he had a sizable following of loyal friends, allies, and voters. He had nurtured these important relationships all along—even through his troubles—and in his time of need they had not deserted him. Because of Barry's ability to cultivate friendships and maintain his relationships, his supporters were able to overlook his human frailties and help him get back on his political feet.

Chapter 11

Little Things Mean a Lot

We must not, in trying to think about how we can make a big difference, ignore the small daily differences we can make, which, over time, add up to big differences that we often cannot foresee.

—Marian Wright Edelman

We are all taught the importance of the common courtesies, the niceties—saying "please," "thank you," "you're welcome." Sadly, in our hustle and bustle world, these acknowledgments get lost and often forgotten as we grow older. However, if you remember to make these "little things" a daily part of your life, you will certainly stand out. Let me give you an example of the results of a simple "thank you."

My agency had the fortunate experience of working with filmmaker Matty Rich in 1992. This very talented young man wrote, produced, directed, and starred in the critically acclaimed film *Straight out of Brooklyn*—at the age of nineteen! Bill Reel, a columnist for *New York Newsday,* devoted an entire column—unsolicited—to the importance of Matty and his stunning debut film. I mentioned to Matty that it would really be nice to acknowledge this effort and suggested we send a thank-you note on a *Straight out of Brooklyn* postcard. The result: this very busy columnist, who rarely takes time out for lunch, let alone press conferences and other events, came to a press conference set up to announce Matty's latest project, directing a feature on a boxing event for TVKO (HBO's sports network) in Atlantic City. Bill said he'd come just to meet Matty because of that thank-you note. Not that he expects them, Bill said, but in his fifteen years in business he had received only three thank-you notes for columns—and Matty's was one of them.

Sending thank-you cards is sooo important! But who takes the time anymore? If you ever read "Dear Abby," you'll notice this is a recurring theme among her letters—complaints from grandmothers/aunts/uncles who never receive thank-you notes from their grandchildren/nieces/nephews. It's a major issue, as it should be. Those kids should send Grandma a note to let her know they received her gift and appreciate the thought. And Grandmas shouldn't forget to practice what they preach—when they receive gifts from the kiddies, they too should properly show their gratitude.

Services rendered should be acknowledged. It's as simple as that. And don't think that once you reach a certain level, you're entitled to neglect your duties. Tom Cruise and his wife, Nicole Kidman, sent thank-you notes to the staff of the U.S. Open after they had enjoyed a day at the tennis matches. Jay Leno, host of the *Tonight* show, sent flowers and cards to all the members of his staff after his first night on the show. (And I'm betting that though David

Letterman has been dubbed the new king of late night, Jay will be around for a long while. He is one of the nicest people in show business and a truly warm, personable man. In fact, he is the only host of a show who ever took the time to talk with me—the "lowly" publicist—when Eddie Murphy was a guest on the show. Usually that job is relegated to the show's producers.) A businesswoman in Atlanta sends thank-you cards for new business referrals that say "Thanks for Helping Us Grow" and notes that a donation was made to a charity in the person's name.

Treating people with a little attentiveness reaps many rewards and opens countless doors. Many people have an apathetic attitude and simply don't think about common courtesies. Yet if more people did care, we would all enjoy a better workplace and a better world. Take the time to do your part and realize that knowing a little something about a person—their concerns or causes—will enable you to connect on a more personal level. If you're willing to take care of the little things, you can come across as a star. Let me give you some examples.

After meeting someone you'd like to stay in touch with, send a follow-up note that says you enjoyed meeting that person. (But do this only if you really did. Your new contact will spot a load of BS a mile away.) Mention a mutual area of interest or something noteworthy about the encounter.

Do favors for people. Again, the gestures must be sincere—everyone has sensitive BS detectors—and if they are, you'll reap rewards beyond the simple satisfaction of doing a good turn.

Tony Wafford, my creative director in Los Angeles, makes it a point to help out a writer who works for a trade magazine. This writer doesn't drive, and anyone who knows Los Angeles knows that driving in that town is a necessity of life—it ranks right up there with eating and breathing. Well, Tony goes out of his way every other week or so to take this writer to the store and on various errands. And I guarantee that this small favor will be remembered by this writer the next time he's trying to decide which story he'll want to write—the one Tony was talking to him about or the three other ideas he has floating around. It's only human that he'll remember what Tony has done for him. Know that when people are inundated with things, they need to begin that "weeding out" process. Tony has developed a nice relationship with the writer—based on a few little "extras" and niceties—that will put him on the "keepers" side of the list.

Let me tell you the power of what a "little thing" like sending a quick note or a card can do for you. A few years ago I sent a letter to Peter Stringfellow, whose clubs by the same name were then the hottest places to be—both in New York and in London. He didn't know me from a hole in the wall, but I had seen him MC an awards program and was taken by his excellent, humorous performance. So I sent him a short note and told him how I admired the work he had done, his entrepreneurial spirit and success, and his stint as master of ceremonies. About a week later he wrote me back and said hello and thanks by giving me a full membership at his clubs in London and New York.

Also make it a point to remember people's birthdays, anniversaries, and other occasions, especially the holidays that are celebrated by your friends of different religions or cultures. (Of course, be sure you know what they celebrate—and in this day and age you certainly can't just guess based on last names or whom someone works for.) When I, as a Black woman, have the presence of mind to remember such holidays as Yom Kippur or Rosh Hashanah, it makes a great impact on my Jewish business associates. My friend Alan Gansberg, a Hollywood TV producer and director, always sends me Kwanza cards during the holidays. The first time he did it, it was hilarious to me because it was so completely unexpected.

If you happen to forget someone's special day, make up for the lapse by sending an extraspecial card or gift on the better-late-than-never plan. We all get busy and tend to procrastinate. But I'll guarantee you that a special card or note will be received warmly *and* remembered—even if it's way overdue. People *will* be astounded that you took the time to do it and were honest and bold enough to admit the delay.

Making time for others will have a profound effect on how you are perceived as a human being—on a personal level *and* in the business world. Be ever mindful and pick up on people's feelings. A perfect example: I once took my cousin Pat and her friends Valerie and Reggie Jackman out to dinner at the Shark Bar, one of the hottest restaurants on Manhattan's Upper West Side (and of which I am a partner). It was a fine meal. Now, most people send flowers as a gesture of thanks—and while that's nice, it really doesn't take a lot of thought, does it? These people were certainly different in saying thanks, and it illustrates the point here perfectly. During dinner they zeroed in on how blown away I was by the music being played that night—the "Philly Sound," that great music that came from the great artists from Philadelphia International (like the O'Jays, Harold Melvin & the Blue Notes, the Stylistics, and Teddy Pendergrass), which I love. So they sent me this tape in a little dollhouse that required a key to open it up. There was a little scroll, and it gave me directions on how to get into this house. And in this little house was this cassette of "Philly Sounds," almost everything that was playing that night during dinner. It was incredible. They had taken time—by picking up on how special that music was to me—to make a little thing like a "thank you" into a well-received big thing.

Or take Brenda, a former executive assistant of mine who—knowing my busy schedule—would volunteer to do things for me that were way above and beyond the call of duty. She would bring in home-cooked food and even offered to do my laundry! (Okay, so the laundry offer was a big thing.) Her gestures, and her ability to zero in on my needs even though I hadn't articulated them to her, simply amazed me. I think she'll always stand out.

Another example of a "little thing" that had great results was shown by a woman in Chicago who was always trying to get in touch with me or talk with me about her work and projects. Because I was so busy, we never really got the chance to do some serious talking. So she came up with what I thought was a simple but brilliant idea. The woman kept in contact with my assistant and would find out when I was going to Chicago. She would then volunteer to pick me up at the airport and would take me wherever I was going. Perfect! I was then a captive audience. It's not as if I were going to jump out of her car, was I? I had to get from point A to point B *somehow*.

In the business world, when you're out with your boss or a client, always watch them and their actions and try to anticipate their needs. They shouldn't have to ask for anything—be a step ahead. If you're accompanying the boss to a meeting, make sure you know the *exact* address of the building you're heading for. Even know which floor the company is on—and take along the phone number of the contact in case something comes up. Remember, you don't *have* to do any of these little things, but if you're really exceptional, you will. And these little things will take only about two minutes out of your day. But that two minutes will make a lasting impression.

The little things can also have an immediate impact on the giver. A psychologist at Cornell University studied the effects small favors had on people. For example, doctors who were brought small gifts from their patients were found to make better medical decisions because the gift put them in a good mood. The research also pointed out that a small token induced pleasant feelings in people and inspired a willingness to help others, helped curb aggression, and improved a person's ability to negotiate, solve problems, and reach decisions.

I'll end this chapter with one final example that shows just how important—and how needed—the little things are. Alan Gansberg, the Emmy Award–winning producer and director in Los Angeles, shared with me the following story about when he was working on his "After School" specials, *My Past Is My Own* and *Crosses on the Lawn*. Alan, terrific human being that he is, would go around each day after shooting and personally thank the cast and crew members for their work. And after each production had wrapped, he wrote notes to all the actors. A "little thing," right?

Well, the point is, hardly anyone does those little things anymore. Alan was made aware of this when his first assistant director relayed to him that the cast members were blown away by his gestures. Michael Warren (the fine actor who used to be on *Hill Street Blues*) even told Alan that in his twenty years in the business, Alan's "thank you" was only the second one he'd ever received from a director. And to further illustrate how rare a simple "thanks" is, a couple of the cast members actually thought that Alan wanted (in some kind of devious way) something from them!

I can also vouch for the power of thank-you notes from the receiving end. I work hard, if I do say so myself, and getting a response to my efforts makes my day. It doesn't have to be long, or elaborate, or especially poetic to work its magic. To wit:

Dearest Terrie:

Thank you so much for the wonderful congrats note *and* the beautiful note cards! I *love* them! So happy you keep in touch.

Love,

Connie Chung

Dear Terrie:

Knowing how vigorously busy you are in building your firm, I am rather astonished that you would take the time to remember my birthday. . . . Thank you for your characteristic thoughtfulness and generosity of spirit.

Thanks again, and I hope you will keep right on building, with the good results that you deserve and, I'm confident, will receive.

Affectionately,

Chester Burger [renowned New York public relations analyst]

Dear Terrie:

Thanks for keeping me informed once again.

Keep swingin',

Wynton Marsalis

Chapter 12

Communication: The Writes and Wrongs

*T*he art of truly communicating with others—in the appropriate format and manner—is a vital aspect of daily living and will help you establish and preserve relationships. Communication takes on many forms. First, and most widely used, of course, is verbal communication. We talk to people all the time—face to face and on the phone. And outside of the occasional "shooting the breeze" or idle chitchat with friends, it's how you talk with people in other, more formal surroundings that will help you succeed. Take note:

You should always try to be as direct as possible—get your point across quickly—and as pleasant as you can be, and be sure to *smile*. Remember that smiling people are perceived as smarter than their frowning friends or co-workers.

When speaking at meetings—either in your own office or outside your place of business—or in public at a seminar, keep in mind the following:

- Prepare yourself: have a firm grasp on the topic you will be talking about. You may want to even practice your speech/points on a friend beforehand to see how you are coming across.

• In business meetings, get across your main point at the beginning of your presentation. Be aware of your audience's body language and facial expressions to make sure that your lead idea has gotten through.

Speak clearly, distinctly, and slowly to grab undivided attention. Sandra Day O'Connor, the first woman to be named to the United States Supreme Court, is known for presenting herself this way. She has said that she trained herself to make people lean forward and pay attention if they wanted to hear what she had to say.

It is very rude to whisper. Leaning over to bend someone's ear automatically excludes everyone else who may be present at the time, making them feel less important and, as a result, alienated. When necessary, you can discreetly and quietly pass along some information to the person next to you. Make sure you have their attention by tapping them on the arm or some other signal, keep your body erect (with maybe a slight nod toward the person), and speak in a low voice so as not to disturb anyone else.

• When speaking in front of a large crowd, know your audience and anticipate their reactions to certain topics. I once was preparing to speak to the players at the NBA Rookie Orientation weekend, which is held every year before the start of the basketball season. I'm a big b-ball fan, and I have a lot of friends who are players and ex-players. So I was quite used to conversing with the guys. However, as I was getting ready to address the rookies, I realized that some of my usual topics, jokes, and anecdotes would go right over their very young heads. I understood that I had to change some things in my speech—my audience was from a different generation.

• Know the official—*and* the unofficial—chain of command by being wary of those who possess real power but may not have the title to go with it. Assistants act as the eyes and ears of their bosses and can often help—or hurt—your cause. Know how to talk to and deal with the assistants or administrative staff. Befriend them, assist them in any way possible, which will help you reach the top person. Remember how my relationship with Eddie Murphy developed? Through his friends and support staff.

Darryl Clark, a film unit publicist who used to work in music publicity (handling megastars like Diana Ross, Michael Jackson, and Richard Pryor), realized the importance of dealing with and recognizing the assistants. He says, "I always knew that the support staff are just as important as anyone at a company. Whenever artists came into our office, I would take them to the mailroom to visit the guys who rarely saw anybody or knew what was going on in the rest of the building. The artists would get a kick out of it, but—more important—the guys in the mailroom would be blown away. And believe me, they told me so—no one else had done that before. And by doing what I did, the guys would always take care of me if I had a big mailing to do or whatever. The thought—the personal touch—was remembered."

Written communication—letters, memos, notes—should always be accurate and error free. Yes, we all make mistakes, and a later chapter will offer advice on what to do when you err. However, it's also important to realize that a letter—unlike verbal communication, where you have the chance to correct a mistake immediately—gets into someone's hands, and you're not there to say "Oh, excuse me, that's really not what I meant. Let me explain."

Therefore, your written correspondence should be grammatically correct and devoid of punctuation and spelling mistakes. Always check your letters for typos, grammar, and sentence structure before they are sent to someone. Nothing irks me more than seeing a letter full of typos and mistakes—especially a letter from an "alleged" business professional. Believe me, nothing sends a quicker negative image of a person than a sloppy, mistake-ridden piece of correspondence. If you have trouble writing a letter, make the effort to better yourself. Take a course; use a "how to" book. Check out the bibliography at the end of this book; I've listed a couple of resource guides that may be helpful.

As with verbal communication, keep your audience in mind; a business letter should be constructed as such and convey the proper tone. An informal dispatch, such as a note between friends or a "just wanted to say hello" letter, can be less structured. Write the way you talk—be conversational. But don't rattle on at the pen/typewriter/computer. Just as a "windbag" who babbles on and on will cause you to lose interest, correspondence that goes on page after page will most likely be tossed aside by the reader. Don't get trapped by the misconception that more is better. All too often, letters, reports, and other written material is measured by its bulk rather than its meaning. Remember that in writing, it's quality vs. quantity. Consider the clear, simple (yet extremely commanding) writing evident in Lincoln's Gettysburg Address (271 words); the Lord's Prayer (66 words); the Declaration of Independence (1,300 words). By contrast, the U.S. government Contractor Management System Evaluation Program was sure to put readers asleep at 38,000 words. I once got a four-page typed letter requesting funds for a nonprofit organization. It went right into the garbage. (It wasn't even fit for bathroom reading—it required too, too much concentration.)

Chapter 13

The Power of the Phone

The telephone—the best communication tool available and probably the most utilized device in any business—can be one of your most important assets. Or it can be a pitfall.

An associate director of training development at New York Telephone (NYNEX) gets peeved when someone answers the phone by saying "Hello, please hold." "Then you're kept waiting forever," she says. "Another thing that bothers me is calling a service company with a question and having to go through five people to get an answer."

In this high-tech world of fax machines, voice mail, and automated message centers, it's a wonder we can even get through to a real, live person. But we must, in order to apply the personal touch. And that's why the absolute, most important, never forget rule of using the telephone is . . . picking it up to *return phone calls*. It's simply rude—I even find it disgusting—not to return phone calls. Therefore, I constantly stress to my staff that they must return every phone call—and do so within a reasonable amount of time.

Sherry Lansing, the head of Paramount Pictures, is known to do whatever it takes to return every call she gets on the same day—even if that means she's dialing the phone at midnight! Jim Baker, former secretary of state and, during the Reagan/Bush years, one of the most powerful persons in Washington, had a long-standing policy of returning every call—even from the merest freshman member of Congress—preferably on the same day. Because of this gesture and the relationships he had strengthened through similar actions, he was a favorite on the Hill, not an easy task in our gridlocked nation's capital.

Peter Bart of *Variety* devoted his whole column once to the importance of returning calls. Seems he had run into a young upstart who had just been raked over the coals by his boss for failing to return calls. The kid complained that the "old farts think that's the most important thing on the agenda. If I called back every has-been . . . I'd never have time to work my own deals."

Bart noticed that one name on the agent's phone log was David Picker and asked whether he was called back. "Who is that?" the kid asked. That's when he learned that David Picker, at one time or another, had been head of production of just about every studio in Hollywood and that he'd just signed a new deal with Paramount and would be making a lot more pictures. When the kid asked, "What's he done lately?" Bart just shook his head, unbelieving, he wrote. His column continued, "Talk to top players in the agency business like Ron Meyer of CAA or Jerry Katzman of the William Morris Agency and they'll tell you they never go home at the end of the day without returning every phone call. It's not just a question of good manners; it's also fulfilling a sort of social contract."

I don't know how far that young agent will go, but I do know how much more successful he would be if he took the time to dial the phone.

One reason for returning all phone calls, and treating everyone the same, is that you never know what the call is—or could be—about. I *never* blow anybody off, and I never discount anybody. If someone tells me they're gonna be a superstar someday, I'll give them the benefit of the doubt. I tell them to go for it! Hey . . . we can't predict the future, and you just never know what will happen. One of the most successful and rewarding campaigns my agency ever handled involved that fabulous a cappella group, TAKE 6. How we came about handling this sensational sextet all started back when I was at Essence. The talented woman who would later become the group's manager called me asking if I could assist in getting Susan Taylor (editor in chief of *Essence*) to speak at an Urban League dinner. Then she told me that she was thinking of getting into talent management—could I help with some advice? I explained that I didn't know all that much and did hook her up with some people who knew more about that business, but I gave her my home phone number and told her she could call whenever she liked.

Later, when she was managing TAKE 6, there was no question as to who would handle their publicity. TAKE 6, of course, became triple Grammy Award winners, and their debut album went gold (helped along by our sensational public relations campaign, if I do say so myself). See what I'm saying? What if I had blown off that woman all those years ago when I didn't know from Adam the voice coming over my telephone receiver?

Here's another thing about returning phone calls and about what the lack of a personal touch can do to you. Linda Stasi, who writes the "Hot Copy" column for the *New York Daily News,* took a hard-line swing—and hit a homer—at Diana Ross in an item about the diva's plan to write her autobiography. Stasi wrote, "Why do celebrities who are dying to pen their stories have publicists who'd rather die than admit it? (Ross is so fabulous, even her publicist won't return calls) . . ." Ouch!

Okay, just one more thing about the phone: "Telephone tag" is a ridiculous waste of time. Leave a time when you can be reached or find out when the person you are calling will be back. And when you're calling busy people at the office or at home, it's more considerate to leave a message as to why you're calling as opposed to just "Please call me . . ." In addition to being polite and helpful, this will allow the person to be prepared with a response when you do connect.

And one more . . . all right, so shoot me. Tony, our L.A. guy, says he's noticed that nine times out of ten when he gets a message that says it's "important," it isn't. Not to him, anyway. Check it out yourself. It may be important to the person who was calling, but I have also found that every time I get an "urgent" message—unless it has to do with a change in that night's scheduled event or something like that—it's not been earth-shatteringly important. Bottom line: Don't say it's urgent or important unless you explain the reason—meaning there must be a reason. The person who rushes to call you back will remember it if they feel they're responding to a false alarm. You've heard the story of the boy who cried wolf?

One *last* thing? . . .

If you are a woman and need to call a man at home (and he lives with a woman or is married), make sure to show a sign of respect, and minimize any chance for suspicion by getting the mate's name and addressing that person should she pick up the phone. Say something like "Hi, Mary. This is Terrie Williams. Is John home?" Or, if you can't get this info beforehand, try this: "Hi, is this John's better half? This is Terrie Williams, and I'm calling to . . ." and give a brief description of your business call. If you're a man who needs to phone a woman, the same procedures should apply. Also show some enlightenment—and respect—for same-sex relationships and follow the same rules. It's all a matter of showing a regard for other folks' feelings.

Okay, the absolute final, no more, last thing. Remember the importance of dealing with staff members? It also applies when talking on the phone. Never "diss" the administrative assistant by not complying with their wishes as to who is calling, the nature of the call, and so on. You must be cognizant that the other person you're trying to reach is very busy and is trying to save time—just as you are—by having an assistant cut to the chase. I *always* leave my first and last name and take the time to explain my reason for phoning. I even tell them what would be a good time for them to reach me.

All right, I lied. Just a couple more points. Don't forget your phone etiquette. Just as you respect people you deal with in person by displaying proper manners, always make it a point to act appropriately on the phone. This means introducing yourself properly, politely asking for your party, developing a clear, pleasant phone voice, and refraining from eating, drinking, and chewing gum while you're on the phone.

Section Three

Reputation

Chapter 14

Reputation

A solid, honorable reputation—like a strong relationship—is created, nurtured, and maintained. It doesn't just appear out of nowhere. It can't be bought, and it won't stand the test of scrutiny or time if it is falsified in any manner. To establish or enhance a good reputation, you must combine a number of character-building ingredients—among them hard work, persistence, honesty, and disdain for mediocrity, as well as the good sense to learn from your mistakes and the ability to become a leader. When these qualities mesh together like pieces of a puzzle, you'll soon realize that for those of good standing there are inexhaustible opportunities for success. More important, everyone you meet will know and recognize that you are a decent, reputable human being. The best kind!

If I had a dollar for every time someone said to me that they had heard or seen something favorable about me or my company . . . well, I could help President Clinton with that nasty old national debt, know what I mean? What people say, see, read, or hear about you personally, and you professionally, is—quite simply—what can make or break you. Flat out. No excuses or explanations necessary. This is your reputation. And if you are to succeed as a person, as a professional, as *anything*, your reputation must be of the highest order.

This section of the book will offer lessons on how to position yourself as a person of character and prestige and will explain why it is so vital to maintain a stellar reputation. We must all remember that in the grand scheme of things, in the final analysis, we have just one thing we can always rely on—our name. My moniker is on the door to my agency. Therefore, in the long run it is my name (as a singular person) and my reputation (as an entrepreneur) that will reap the rewards of a job well done—or suffer the indignities of failure.

> *To be meek, patient, modest, honorable, brave, is not to be either manly or womanly. It is to be humane.*
>
> —JANE HARRISON, ENGLISH SCHOLAR

In the inspiring book *Think and Grow Rich: A Black Choice,* Dennis Kimbro wrote: "Every person is in business for himself; that is, he is building his own life regardless of who signs his paycheck. Within a free and open society, all of us are entrepreneurs. Each of us, individually, is the president of his or her own corporation. As you assume this office, you, and you alone, are solely responsible for your firm's success or failure."

Don't let the "business/president" metaphor scare you. We are not talking literally of going into business for yourself. But the bottom line is you *own* your actions, your decisions, your successes or failures. They make or break you, as surely as a CEO's actions determine the fate of a company. But you are captain of your own ship. Regardless of your circumstances or origins, you can achieve anything you set out to do. Success is measured not by where you start out in life, but by how far you go. Nor is success measured by the fleeting trappings of wealth—cars, money, gold chains, whatever. They can all be gone tomorrow. Most of all, it is important not to compare yourself with others. You could go nuts trying to do that. Draw inspiration from them, definitely. But do not let jealous comparisons get in your way.

Instead, as my friend Susan Taylor says, compare yourself with who you were and where you were last week, last month, last year. (That's the real measure of success and enhancing your reputation.) And strive to move forward. Let me give you a couple examples of how your reputation can help or hurt you.

Chester Burger, a giant in the public relations industry, was one of my first mentors, guides, and instructors in the PR business. Whenever I had a question or problem, I knew that I could call on Chet and he would be there for me. I remember one time when Chet had asked me to meet with a guy who was looking for a job. Now, I would do anything for Chet when asked, so I agreed without question. However, when he told me the name of the guy I was to talk with, I couldn't believe it. Turns out it was a columnist I had been reaching out to for over two years when I was at Essence. And I had never heard a peep out of him, although I did hear through the grapevine that he was sometimes disreputable. So when I did indeed call him—as a favor to Chet—I let the guy know what I thought of his previous (non)actions. Nicely, of course. He made some feeble excuses. Didn't cut it, and I told him so. He hadn't had time to nurture or even establish contact with me before. And then look what happened. I told him if I heard of anything I'd let him know, but in my eyes, his reputation had been sullied long ago. That's why it pays to treat everyone with respect and courtesy. Know that your reputation is your most important asset and that it can and will make a difference. You never can tell.

On the flip side: A couple of years ago when I provided PR counsel to the mayor of Washington, D.C., Sharon Pratt Kelly, a reporter from *The Washington Post* phoned to say she was doing a story on me—as an outsider who would be advising the mayor of the district. I immediately got the feeling that this was going to be one of those "what's the dirt on this person/just who is this/she can't be all *that*" articles, since the reporter talked to all kinds of people—colleagues, associates, reporters, former staffers, competitors, and so on—about me and my business. And you know what? The "exposé" turned out to be a glowing feature—I couldn't have paid for that kind of positive publicity. The bottom line: When you try your best to do things right, your reputation remains more or less intact *and* you have protectors out there in the universe. Your good deeds protect you to a great extent, and people tend not to focus on your bad habits, traits, or skeletons—'cause we all got 'em. It's a variation on the "what goes around, comes around" theme.

Another story was done on me once, and the writer shared with me that the editor on the piece had specifically asked her to talk to people (ex-employees) who would discuss some of my not-so-virtuous qualities. The writer refused. (It wasn't that these traits didn't exist or that the article was intended to be a "puff" piece—it's just that the story was a celebration of my accomplishments, and the writer knew it served no point to dredge up any dirt.)

Remember, too, that your reputation—good or bad—follows you forever. When high-profile sports agent Bob Woolf died in 1993, nearly every newspaper story on his death mentioned his stellar reputation. Woolf was always a man of integrity, honesty, and cordiality (the personal touch!), which made him something of a rarity in a cutthroat business in which agents are known for sometimes caring more for their percentages than for the athletes they represent. Woolf was different. His clients—and even his adversaries—admired and respected him.

Chapter 15

Hard Work

When Harry Truman became president of the United States, few people expected much from a man who came from such a humble background. Yet just a few years later, Winston Churchill was calling him the man who saved Western civilization. Truman got to the White House without the help of inherited wealth, influential family connections, superior education, or personal glamour.

But Truman ascribed to a way of life that was steeped in traditional values—hard work, persistence, loyalty, honesty, and self-reliance. He put everything he had into his work—and his life. And his achievements were unparalleled. Known to rise early and work late into the night, Truman tackled all his jobs with vigor. When serving in the Senate, he arrived so early that he became the first senator to be issued a key to the building. As a young man he had a long record of failure, yet he never let the fear of failure discourage him. There was never a book or collection of "kiss and tell" memoirs written by someone close to Truman because he inspired a lasting allegiance in those who knew him and worked for him. He was true to his family, his friends, and himself. He always treated people as people. He was never afraid to take advice, but when the time came for action he always made the decisions himself. Think about the famous phrase that is synonymous with Truman: "The buck stops here." Think about it, learn from it. Live it.

This man of many values, despite his unassuming background, was the president who, among many other history-making accomplishments, ended segregation in the U.S. military and the federal Civil Service; introduced the strategy of containment of the old Soviet Union; pushed the Marshall Plan to rebuild Western Europe. Harry Truman will forever be known as one of the most influential and important leaders of the world. Why? Because his work ethic was one of dedication and determination. Look up "hard work" in the dictionary and you should find Truman.

I came across an inspiring story awhile back about an African-American woman by the name of Bessie Pender, who epitomized the essence of hard work. For seventeen years this woman worked as a custodian helper at an elementary school outside Washington, D.C. Every day she and a partner cleaned seventeen classrooms each, four bathrooms, three offices, and the teachers' lounge. She would head home at nine at night, exhausted from a full day's work. All the while, she was going to college part-time.

Two days after signing another year-long contract as a custodian—her eighteenth—Pender got a call from the principal of a neighboring elementary school. And when she put down the phone she screamed with joy, dropped her bucket and mop, and received congratulations from her co-workers as well as the teachers. Pender had just been informed that she'd been hired to teach the fifth grade at the public school. It took seven years of part-time schooling for the woman to earn her degree in education. During that time, she also volunteered as a teacher's aide, and would correct papers and do bulletin boards.

Now, as a full-time teacher, Pender works all weekend preparing her class assignments and lesson outlines. She is strict with the children, but also caring, praising, and full of humor. And at day's end her classroom is still clean because, she said, "I try to help the custodians."

There's another lesson here: The principal of the school where she cleaned had not offered the woman a teaching job. She thought it best that Pender not teach there because she felt the students would not be able to "see" Pender as anything but a cleaning lady. I think instead that Pender would have made a great role model. The lesson to the children: Look at what's possible. With persistence and plain old-fashioned hard work, you can do anything!

The educational system in this country could certainly use teachers like this inspirational woman. The world, too, would surely benefit if everyone had this woman's drive and determination.

Giving an all-out effort doesn't seem to be as popular today as it was years ago. This may explain why so few people climb that ladder of success to heights above the ranks—and why I agree with other leaders in the industry that it's easier to succeed today. Too many people, in any industry or scope of life, find it easier to submerge themselves in mediocrity. They find comfort in conforming, a sense of security in the daily routine. But this can be overcome.

Give (your all—and more) and you shall receive. It's a lot like what we said before: What goes around, comes around. Giving to others—your time, your honesty, your service, your productivity, your commitment, and your loyalty—will result in the enhancement of you and your reputation. I've often been called—at the very last minute—to travel on behalf of a client or to fill in for someone at a dinner, seminar, or speaking engagement. Sure, some of those times I've had to drag my ass out of bed, dog tired and just not in the mood. But I do go. It's my calling, plain and simple. The work that comes with a "calling" may not be plain nor simple. But if you want to succeed . . .

So I go, and I give it all that I've got. In fact, you should be—as I am—ready to go in a flash. I wear very little makeup, and I prefer a haircut that makes me look practically bald. Therefore I'm ready in five minutes to head out the door if you call me and say I need to be somewhere. There are people I know—people I deliberately won't invite someplace—because I only have 15 minutes' notice and I know it will take that person a good hour or two to get ready to go someplace. I'm sure you know people like that. If you're slow, you blow! Not only will your reputation suffer (you'll be labeled a non-go-getter or worse), but you could miss out on an important opportunity.

Hard work will always be rewarded. And if you truly want to succeed, remember what Don Hewitt, creator and executive producer of television's legendary *60 Minutes*, says:

"I don't know the formula for success. But I do know the formula for failure: resting on your laurels."

Chapter 16

Performance Counts

*T*hose who have worked with me throughout the years will certainly agree that my work ethic is . . . different, let's say. Some would say demanding, others tyrannical. I'm no day at the beach, but I would never ask anyone to do anything I wouldn't do. It all has to do with performance. And I'm reminded of the distinction sometimes used when comparing women and men in the workplace: When a man is overdemanding, he's perceived as "tough" and a leader, a general; when a woman acts the same way, she's labeled "an aggressive bitch." Well, if I'm a "bitch" sometimes, it's because I simply will not succumb to mediocrity. My work ethic and performance is built upon the fact that I take great pains to ensure that everything I do is done to perfection—or as close to perfection as possible. If you truly want to succeed, everything you do must be way above "average." Mediocrity won't cut it.

I learned an important lesson about mediocrity way back when I was first starting out in the communications business. I had sent out my résumé to numerous people at various companies. Any response, of course, was welcomed, and an interview was icing. But I had one interview that truly had a surprise ending. Leslie Lillien, who was then publicity director at WABC-TV, interviewed me and—after I had been turned down for the job—called to say why I hadn't gotten the position. This incredibly busy woman had taken it upon herself to point out the "error of (some of) my ways." Or, in this case, my résumé, which she explained was just short of professional standards. It really struck me that of all the personnel directors, managers, and executives I had contacted in my job search, just one person thought enough, and cared enough, to offer some constructive criticism.

It was an indelible lesson, and it's the reason I'm a real stickler for accuracy today and why I'm so quick to point out—and correct—any error I come across, including my own. If I receive a letter or a résumé that is really bad, I'll circle all the mistakes and send it back to the person with a note: "I hope you'll accept this in the spirit in which it's meant . . . someone once pulled my coat on something like this, and I wanted to do the same."

Leslie certainly stood out and made a difference for me. It's not often a stranger will take the time to say "Look, the way you're doing this—or have done that—is not quite right. You may want to try such-and-such." Take the time to be honest and open with people—don't talk about them behind their back. Just think about it. Wouldn't you want to know? Sometimes (most of the time, actually) it's painful to hear criticism. But (all together now): "If it doesn't kill you, it makes you stronger." And there are very few cases when criticism is known to be fatal.

Not failure, but low aim is sin.
—Dr. Benjamin Elijah Mays

Be careful. And be aware. Nine times out of ten, mediocrity is the result of carelessness, inattention, or ignorance. Perfection, or a result that is as close to perfection as you can get, will come about when you think things through before acting or reacting, keep an eye out for details, concentrate on what you are doing, and know all you can about the task at hand. I am a real stickler for neatness, especially when we photocopy material—I just cannot accept messy copies. And I make sure that every copy we send out of the office is as clean as possible. Once, the Agency had just started working on a new account, and the client had asked for some material to be copied and sent to him. It so happened that our copy machine was not working properly that day, and the copy we made for him was not up to my standards. I didn't want to send them out and wouldn't have, but I did—only because of the urgency. Wouldn't you know: our client calls me right away after receiving the material we sent him and says something along the lines of "Uh, Terrie . . . we want to start off on the right foot, right? Well, these copies you sent me are unacceptable." I knew it! And I made sure to tell him that although there was really no excuse, the copy had been faxed because he'd needed the material so quickly.

The point is, when you're doing something, do it right. Sloppy performance in whatever you do will severely hamper your chances to succeed. Mistakes will cost you. The editor who worked with me on this book says it's one of her pet peeves. Every week she gets tons of submissions—many of them unsolicited—from hopeful authors. How does she sort through all the material and decide what will get read? First she looks for errors. If the stuff comes with an incorrect name, title, and/or address (her company moved two years, and she still gets things sent to her at the wrong address), it goes back immediately with a form rejection letter. She simply will not publish someone who can't even get a few basic facts right.

How do we ensure that our performance is above and beyond the normal call of duty? How can we know that our reputation is being properly built and maintained? Unfortunately, there is no single rule to follow, no secret formula, no one-step system. It is an ongoing process, dictated by everyday actions and gestures. No matter who you are or what you do, your actions speak for themselves—and for you and your reputation. I know I always look at someone's actions and their body language to hear what they don't say. I guarantee you that their actions, or nonactions, will say at least as much as their lip service.

Your actions say more about you and your work ethic than anything you can say about yourself. Do you ever make promises you know you can't, or don't plan to, keep? Are you constantly telling people that you'll "have to get back to them" because you haven't delivered what was promised on time? Do you even get back to them? Do you return phone calls promptly? Acknowledge letters?

We have some rules at the Agency:

1. Meet the deadline.
2. If you can't meet the deadline, *always* acknowledge and explain the delay.
3. Meet the new deadline.

In this fast-paced, hurry-up world, where everyone wants something yesterday, you must be prepared to give your all, when you're supposed to give it.

If you're looking into something for someone and it's going to take you a few days or longer than expected, call and tell the person that you're working on it. Such courtesy is *always* greatly appreciated, and they know you've not forgotten about them. Even when dealing with colleagues—and especially your bosses—always advise them as to when to expect the material you are working on.

How many times have you been out and, in the course of a "schmoozing" conversation, someone has promised to call you, do something for you, send you some info? Then a month goes by and you suddenly realize that you never did hear from the person. So you just chalk it up to another instance of idle, insincere chatter. Don't let your reputation suffer because of vacant promises made in the heat of the networking moment. I can't begin to tell you how many times people have said to me: "You said you were gonna do something . . . but I never thought that you *actually would* do it!" Make a difference. Most people say they'll do something but never get around to it. The next time you're conversing with someone and offer some assistance . . . do it!

Once your performance level is "up there," your reputation will be enhanced and—ultimately and ideally—your colleagues, friends, and even your competitors will come to respect and admire you and your work. And before you know it, you'll be on top. You'll be a leader. So you must be prepared.

In an essay titled "The Penalty of Leadership," Theodore F. MacManus offers many insights on the pros and cons of being a leader. In part, he writes:

> In every field of human endeavor, he that is first must perpetually live in the white light of publicity. Whether the leadership be vested in a man or in a manufactured product, emulation and envy are ever

> at work. In art, in literature, in music, in industry, the reward and the punishment are always the same. The reward is widespread recognition; the punishment, fierce denial and detraction. If his work be merely mediocre, he will be left alone. If he achieve a masterpiece, it will set a million tongues a-wagging . . . If the leader truly leads, he remains the leader. Master poet, master painter, master workman, each holds his laurels through the ages. That which is good or great makes itself known no matter how loud the clamor of denial. That which deserves to live, lives.

Be prepared to be a leader. When possible, lead with your reputation, and remember that your reputation is synonymous with your actions. Uphold, as I always try to do, the universal truths: fairness, equality, justice, honesty, sincerity, and compassion. These principles will help you achieve success in life. Dare to face the "penalties of leadership."

A leader (read: successful person) takes the time for someone. Leslie Lillien's advice has always stuck with me. And from that one phone call from a busy woman—who didn't have to care about me or my résumé—I started to learn that there are a number of essential qualities you must possess if you want to succeed and garner a stellar reputation. These attributes include being sincere and honest; doing what you say you're going to do, *when* you're supposed to do it; and always be prepared. Heed the preceding examples, remember that your reputation is your most valuable possession, and never forget that people are always watching you and your work.

As I said at the beginning of this chapter, I'm often reminded of just how closely the eyes of others are upon me and my agency. But if your shit's together, and if you're giving it your all, the results are these:

Dear Terrie & Staff:

You were terrifically helpful with coverage of the Murphy/Mitchell wedding—cooperative, patient, knowledgeable—and everyone standing behind the press barriers knew it.

I can't remember being in a mob of video crews, photographers, and reporters and hearing words of praise for PR people. Last night, I did.

Now if only we could have put you in charge of the weather . . .

Thanks,

Paula Span [staff writer, *Washington Post*]

Terrie:

Thank you so much for the *House Party* tickets. It was great!

You and your staff did a *wonderful* job. It was one of the most organized affairs I've been to in a long time. Thanks again.

Best,

Jimmy Hester [New York publicist who handles model Beverly Johnson, among others]

Chapter 17

Honesty Is the Best Policy

Care more for the truth than what people think.

—Aristotle

A few years back, the head of a Los Angeles–based publicity firm and I had been in regular contact for quite a while. During that time, my firm was approached by representatives of New Edition, one of the hottest recording groups around. The group was looking to retain our services for public relations, and we did eventually sign them on. Then I found out that the group had been handled by the same Los Angeles firm my contact was a partner of, Levine/Schneider. So I immediately sent off a note to Mitch Schneider, saying that I didn't want him to think that all the while we were keeping in touch I was going behind his back to secure New Edition. It wasn't like that.

Mitch was simply blown away. No one, especially a

competitor, had ever reached out to him like that. He thought it was tremendously classy. (And he didn't hold my new business against me. He didn't hold a grudge because he knows that in this business clients are always switching agencies, and my note made sure everything was cleared up.)

We went on to establish a solid, continuing relationship and even worked together on a few accounts, including a pretty well-known talent by the name of Janet Jackson. And we established an affiliation with Levine/Schneider, a reciprocal "joining of forces" that was beneficial to both companies. My agency acts as the New York eyes and ears for Levine/Schneider; they do the same for us in Los Angeles.

When President Clinton, in early 1993, appointed Janet Reno U.S. attorney general, the woman immediately faced an agenda of problems and situations that would have taxed even the strongest-willed individual. By far the most pressing crisis Reno had to confront was the Waco, Texas, standoff between government agents and David Koresh's Branch Davidians religious sect. Four agents had been killed already in a botched raid on the Koresh compound, and the man who called himself a messiah—along with about eighty-five members of his clan—had kept law enforcement officials at bay for almost two months. Reno finally gave the okay for agents once again to move into the compound; the result was later referred to as "Ranch Apocalypse," an inferno that reduced the compound, and every man, woman, and child in it, to a pile of smoldering ashes.

Of course, Reno's tactics came under heavy scrutiny and attack. During a House Judiciary Committee hearing two weeks after the disaster, Reno was barraged by members of Congress. One even declaimed the outcome at Waco was "a profound disgrace to law enforcement in the United

States." Reno, however, did not back down. She stuck to her guns—as she had since the first flames were seen at the compound. She stood tall, owning up to her actions, and took full responsibility. This show of honesty—in the face of overwhelming adversity—captivated the city of Washington. One prominent lawyer at the time even went so far in his adulation to say, "I predict she'll be such a good attorney general that she'll end up on the Supreme Court."

You may say to yourself—as you may have said to others—"But I *am* sincere, I *am* honest. Honest." Of course you are, and surely that's what you want to get across. But how can you prove it to me or someone else? A friend who owns a small restaurant and bar once related his experiences about hiring bartenders. That's a high-turnover position, so he was often interviewing prospective barkeeps—and there are always hundreds of eager "mixologists" looking for a job at any given time. Through the years the owner found that those applicants who would go to great lengths to *explain* their honesty, usually weren't. "Like what are they going to say?" the owner ponders. "That they're dishonest? Invariably, the ones who made a big deal about it were the most trouble. So I've learned to rely solely on references. If they've done honest work in the past, if they have a good reputation, I'll hire them."

Honesty also means being up-front and open with people, on a personal level. If there's something I observe about someone I care about that is offensive or not cool or unprofessional, I have a responsibility to tell my friend about his or her actions. If I'm inclined to talk of it to another person, that would be talking behind my friend's back. I can't (and won't) do that and still be able to call myself a friend of that person.

In the same spirit, I always include in my talks at industry seminars, universities, and the like a story I refer to as "the spinach in the teeth" example. It's all about being aware of what's going on around you and being honest with yourself and with others. The example: If you see someone who has a piece of food (spinach) in his/her teeth—or whose slip is showing, or whose zipper is down—let that person know! I know I wouldn't want to be walking around at an event some night grinning in your face the whole time, only to get home later and find out that I had a sliver of spinach stuck in my teeth. (And I'll know you saw it and didn't tell me!) Maybe I'm crazy, but I just don't understand how you can see something like that and not pull a person's coat about it.

It's about connecting on a personal, human level. And if you can be blunt, and open, and honest, more often than not it makes everyone feel more comfortable. I remember once having a conference call with the publicity team at a film studio. My agency was being hired to handle the part of the campaign that would target the African-American market. The studio people and I were discussing the PR strategies for the film, and the assignments for all involved were being distributed. One man, whom I had not met in person yet, kept hesitating a bit when the conversation turned to the duties the Agency would be handling. I could sense he was having a bit of trouble—he kept starting and stopping: "Okay, Terrie, you'll handle . . . Ummm, your people will take care of . . . Uh, the Agency will target . . ."

I finally blurted out to him, "It's okay. We'll handle the *Black* stuff." He was obviously trying to make sure he wouldn't offend me in any way, and I just had to point out the obvious and honest fact: what we were hired to do. Everyone laughed, and my comment certainly broke the tension, and the rest of the call went smoothly.

Learn to be open and honest with people. It will help you connect on a better, more personal level.

Chapter 18

Admitting (and Learning from) Your Mistakes

*A*t The Terrie Williams Agency, we have what we call the "happily" letter. Should we find a typo, or other mistake in any correspondence that has already gone out to someone, we make sure to send a corrected version, along with a letter that begins, "Happily, it's not often that we must send a letter such as this. But when required, we do so with a sense of duty. . . ."

This little bit of humble pie that we have to swallow every so often (more often than I'd like, actually, but nobody's perfect) shows that we are simply human. Everyone makes mistakes. We surely do our best to avoid the blunders, but when they do occur we admit to them, move swiftly to correct them, and—hopefully—learn from them. That's what separates us from others. In fact, we even point out this little practice when we are meeting with potential clients for the first time, because they always seem to find our candor and sincerity refreshingly different.

Once a new client of ours got a memo from us that contained a couple of typos. We caught the mistakes about a day later and faxed off our little "happily" letter, along with a corrected copy of the memo. The client, Lori Shackel from the L.A.-based ITC Entertainment Group, told me later that she had actually gone back into her files to find the original memo because she hadn't even noticed the typos. Lori told us she really appreciated our efforts. She even pointed out that in all the years she had been in business, she had experienced only one other similar apology, from someone who had sent her correspondence that contained errors. After discovering the mistakes, the person sent Lori an elaborately designed cutout/stand-up card depicting a teacher slapping a student's knuckles for making a mistake. The copy read:

> Ouch! We made a terrible mistake. We misspelled your name. We didn't know you got married. It was an oversight, a screw-up, and ouch, did it hurt. But true to our professional form, Lori (see, it's sinking in), we're taking full responsibility for our error. Thanks for understanding. As you can see, our knuckles aren't the only things that are red!

Needless to say, Lori was also impressed with them and went on to give them more business.

The public relations business is full of ups and downs, highs and lows. We are in the service business; we're hired to help our clients. Should our level of service fall below our expectations—and not necessarily the client's desires, but our standard 120 percent effort—I take it personally. So as soon as there is the slightest hint of a problem, we act on it and look for a solution. We'll try to do some extra things for the client, even extend our campaign—at no charge. We once worked a book account on which we, sad to say, didn't produce as much as we would have liked. I knew we didn't demonstrate the excellence we are known for on that one, but I kept in touch with the author of the book and sent him articles on a topic that was somewhat related to his work. We screwed up, but I wanted him to know we cared. Turns out he was most appreciative, because he was writing another piece—for a magazine article—on the same topic. The point is: If you lose a job or mishandle an assignment—even if you get fired—go out with style. Don't burn bridges. Admit your mistakes and learn from them. There is strength to be gained from adversity, and when you make the effort to right a wrong, your courage will be noticed and your reputation enhanced.

Chapter 19

Perception Is Reality

*W*e have seen how your reputation can enhance your success. A close cousin of your reputation is the image you project. We'll start at the beginning here. How do you "appear" to those you interact with, to those you are meeting for the first time? As the saying goes, "You never get a second chance to make a first impression." And while you may be able to rectify a negative first impression, why not get it right the first time?

Always be aware of how you come across to other people. If you're not sure, find out. It may be a painful lesson, but it is worth enduring. You'll be a better person for it. About five or six years ago I took a human awareness course called LifeSpring. At one point during the intense five-day program we were asked to pair off with another person. One exercise we did involved having the other person act out what they thought about their partner. So my partner, Will Farquhar, takes my pocketbook, flings it over his shoulder, and walks around the room—the three hundred people in the class witnessed this—with his nose up in the air. His observation was that I was aloof and distant. I was like "Whoa, wait a minute." I always considered myself a pretty friendly, down-to-earth person. Where was this coming from? I asked a few other people in the class what they thought about his impression—and they agreed with my partner's assessment. They pointed out that when we took breaks I would go off by myself and not mingle. Truth of the matter is I'm very shy, and I was afraid to walk up to people and introduce myself. Had it been a business situation, I would have had no qualms about "working" the room. But this wasn't work, and my inhibitions implied to the others that I was "distant." Sure, my feelings were hurt by the experience. But it was enlightening and important to me to know how people perceived me. Perception is reality! It didn't matter what *I* thought. What an invaluable lesson!

The first thing a person will notice about you is your appearance. And believe me, your appearance will implant an immediate impression—and perception of you—into someone's mind. If you want to be the congenial slob in the old, tattered suit, wrinkled shirt, and stained tie who just wants to make friends in the hole-in-the-wall bar down the street, well, that's your decision. But know that you certainly wouldn't be welcome or respected in a business meeting. Remember that personal grooming cannot be taken lightly.

Men: make sure your suit is pressed, your shirts crisp and unstained, your shoes shined. Ladies: it ain't Saturday night every day, know what I mean? "Dress to impress" means one thing on club night and another during working hours. We adhere to a dress policy at the Agency, yet on Fridays—especially during the summer—we relax it and go casual. But it's stressed that everyone must still be prepared to meet with a client, go to an unexpected meeting, attend a business function—whatever—even at the last minute. That means all staff members need to have a change of clothes in the office for just such occasions. If a representative of the Agency is out of line—in attire or demeanor—it reflects on me. I simply can't have that happen. Remember, everybody is watching. Or as the incredibly successful author Stephen King once wrote: "Perfect paranoia is perfect awareness."

Evaluate your own clothes and "style." Know that what you wear and how you present yourself can open many doors and have an immediate impact on those you meet. Tony Wafford, the Agency's man in Los Angeles, has an incredible wardrobe and is always looking as if he just stepped out of a *GQ* photo spread. And he gets complimented on this time and time again. I realized just how important certain things, in terms of clothes and accessories, are when I observed how folks responded to Tony. And because he dresses the way he does, people who meet him automatically perceive him to be someone they can deal and work with.

To prove the point: Tony and I once accompanied a client to the "I Have a Dream" organization Christmas party. Jonathan Tisch, one of the most influential and powerful businessmen in the country and head of the Loews Hotel chain, was attending with his wife, Laura. (The party was hosted by Jonathan's in-laws, Saul & Gayfryd Steinberg.) I introduced Tony to Jonathan at one point during the afternoon; Tisch took a look at Tony, and I saw him notice the nice suit, sharp-looking shirt and designer tie, and the kicker: alligator shoes. Jonathan made a comment on the shoes, and they began a conversation.

Tony was immediately perceived and received in a positive manner because of his exquisite taste in clothes and outstanding personal appearance. Your wardrobe can instantly convey the right (or wrong) image of who you are and what you do. An impeccable wardrobe stands out, is noticed, and is often the "icebreaker" that enables you to meet or talk with other people. Actor David Hasselhoff, from TV's *Baywatch*, once was sitting across from Tony on a flight to Los Angeles and started a conversation with him that began with a comment on his shoes! (Are you getting tired of hearing about Tony's shoes?)

Similarly, that's why I make a point of carrying a Mont Blanc pen. Yes, they're expensive (especially because I lose them all the time), but it's the kind of detail that impresses the hell out of people.

It should be a given that proper grooming and attire is adhered to by all in the business world. However, you can relax your style a bit once you reach a certain stature—and are positive that your reputation precedes you. Rap impresario Russell Simmons, chairman of RUSH Communications, may show up at a formal event with his ever-present baseball cap (worn backward, of course) and his high-tops. But that's okay—Russell's body of work, his musical savvy, and his reputation (oops, I almost forgot—and his deep pockets) speak for him. Sometimes I'll go to business meetings dressed a little bit more casually than might normally be accepted, but I know that I am one of the best at what I do and this is the way I dress. And if someone doesn't want to hire me because I don't want to put on a dress and stockings (I hate stockings) . . . well, so be it. Sure, when I was starting out I'd don the appropriate business suit or whatever. But now that I have established myself, I've reached a certain level, and I wear what is comfortable for me. Keep in mind, too, the accepted "industry standards." If you are working for a record company, jeans and T-shirts may be the normal style of dress. Of course, faded Levi's wouldn't cut it in a more formal business environment, such as a bank.

Your clothing can be an asset to you in your efforts to stand out. Your individual style can become a trademark for you and your work. Novelist Tom Wolfe is instantly recognizable in his white suit. No matter what the season, no matter where he is, Wolfe always wears white. Or how about Diane Keaton? The "Annie Hall" look became a worldwide fashion rage. The charismatic Vernon Jordan is always impeccably dressed—and his ever-present boutonniere is his personal signature. I am known for my flowing, colorful pants, dresses, and coats and exotic, hanging earrings.

Try to develop your own style or look. It will help you stand out, get noticed, and be remembered. Combined with your reputation, honesty, and being a "people person," your sense of style will lead people to perceive you as a successful and worthy professional.

Chapter 20

Persistence

To tend, unfailingly, unflinchingly, towards a goal, is the secret of success.

—Anna Pavlova

*P*ersistence is the quality that separates those who make it from those who don't. Simply put: Those who make it stayed in the race. You can't win if you don't finish. Anyone can be persistent. It's as easy as "Don't quit." Of course, quitting is easy. Anyone can do that, too. But if you truly want to make a difference, you must challenge yourself constantly and never give up. Earl Graves, founder and publisher of *Black Enterprise* magazine, often relates a story about when he went to work for Robert Kennedy, then a New York senator. Graves found himself in an unfamiliar world where power was a natural heritage and the word *can't* did not exist.

Graves has said that "Robert Kennedy was a man who was totally unfamiliar with failure."

The senator once asked Graves to reach Secretary of the Interior Udall. Udall was on vacation at the time, on a rafting expedition in Colorado. Graves tried numerous times—all unsuccessfully—to reach the secretary. When he relayed this information to the senator, Kennedy responded sternly, "Graves, that raft is not going down the river all day. It's going to stop somewhere. And when it does I want Udall standing there with a phone in his hand."

Kennedy expected Graves to find a way. Graves says today, "That story is a part of my personal philosophy. You'd be surprised how many people quit when faced with obstacles." Indeed, Graves has applied this maxim for over twenty-four years as he has kept *Black Enterprise* one of the country's top business publications.

Comedian Joan Rivers is a prime study in persistence. Way back when, she reportedly auditioned for the *Tonight* show no less than six times before she finally got a chance to appear. Of course, she eventually went on to become one of the regular substitute hosts of the program before she and Johnny (Carson) had their infamous falling-out. All this is on top of the personal challenges she has faced—including the suicide of her husband—yet she has always found a way to become one of the most successful women in television.

John Starks never quit. He just knew that someday he would play professional basketball. Inside himself, he knew he had the talent. Equally important, he had the drive. Even after high school, when he was passed over by the college scouts, he wouldn't let that deter him, so he played for a couple of junior colleges in his hometown of Tulsa, Oklahoma. He supplemented his income by bagging groceries at the local supermarket. Eventually he was picked up by a pro team, but he hardly ever played. Then he tried out for a spot on another team but was sidelined by an ankle injury almost immediately. He ended up in the Continental Basketball Association, the minor league of basketball.

Yet, "I never thought about quitting," he says. "Never." He was then picked up by the Knickerbockers in New York and finally—with a healthy body and the right chance—proved that he was a bona fide player, even a star! In the 1992–93 season he helped lead the Knicks to the league's best record in the regular season and to the finals of their division playoffs.

Another example of someone who knows what it means to persist is that of a woman named Ree Adler, who at the age of 52 became one of the oldest first-year students at the State University of New York Law School in Buffalo. For Adler, going to law school required the courage to break away from a happy yet ultimately unfulfilling life of marital domesticity.

It wasn't easy for a middle-aged woman to go back into the classroom. But Adler confronted her fears and the skepticism and persisted. A student in her law class once said to her: "I *have* to do this, but why are you doing it?" Adler responded, "I have to do it, too. I need to be me, not just somebody's wife or mother."

As a lawyer who now works for the Neighborhood Legal Services in Buffalo, Adler continues to be daring and bold. She once defied all legal procedures when battling the Social Security Administration on behalf of a client who had a kidney transplant. Social security paid for the operation but would not pay for the drugs the patient needed to survive. Adler was angry, so she called up the president of the company that made the drug and told him the story. He replied that he couldn't provide drugs free of charge for everybody. Adler told him that she wasn't asking him to do it for everybody, just for this one person.

Something about the way she said it must have hit a nerve with the guy: the patient now has a lifetime supply of the life-saving drugs.

Let me relate another success story filled with persistence: Mike Krzyzewski (and I think *I* have problems getting people to spell my name right!) is a true champion among champions because of the way he has conducted himself. As head coach of the Duke University basketball team, he never gave up, even under great pressure and difficult challenges, and he held true to a life-style that revolved around his good qualities. During his first four seasons at Duke, his team had a losing record. But he still believed he could change that. He persevered, believed in himself, and convinced others to believe in him. His contract was renewed, and the next season was indeed a winning one. He eventually won two national championships. Krzyzewski is also a man of integrity: he made sure that the members of his team studied the books as well as the *X's* and *O's*. As a result, most, if not all, of the players have graduated and even gone on to obtain advanced degrees. That's highly unusual in a situation where many sports-obsessed universities don't care if a valuable player makes the grades as long as he makes the baskets. And in 1990, when the team won the national championship, Krzyzewski refused to raise the banner in the team's gymnasium. Why? Because two of his players had yet to complete their academic requirements for that season. Above all, Krzyzewski—like legendary figures Eddie Robinson, John Thompson, and John Chaney—is a human being. He's not only coach to his players, he's a mentor, a friend, and a father figure. That's the personal touch. He cares and respects them as people first, players second. In return, his players have always given him their best.

Chapter 21

Creativity

Persistence is an attribute that can be self-taught. But creativity can be a complex and hard-to-grasp quality. It's not impossible, however. Some people *are* more creative than others, but does this mean that they are more intelligent, or better educated? Not necessarily.

Bill Backer, president and executive creative director of the huge advertising agency Backer Spielvogel Bates, has written a book called *The Care and Feeding of Ideas*. Backer explains the various thought processes—designed to nurture and maintain good ideas—he has used as guidelines throughout his successful professional life. And when I say successful, I mean it. This guy has an incredible track record. To wit: The advertisement touting "It's Miller Time" was Backer's idea. So was the enormously popular campaign for Miller Lite beer: "Tastes Great, Less Filling." That campaign, with legions of sport stars in humorous ads, helped turn Miller Lite into one of the best-selling beers of all time. And remember the legendary Coca-Cola hilltop singers commercial, with the song "I'd like to buy the world a Coke"? That was Backer's creation also. The man has enjoyed a fabulously lucrative career by being creative.

Backer isn't superhuman, though. Nor does he possess the ability to conjure up best-selling ad campaigns whenever he feels like it. He works at it. He gets to know his subject, stays on top of trends, listens to others, and—as an added plus—is persistent.

Imaginative or inventive ideas can also come about by looking beyond the ordinary, doing the unusual or unexpected, and thinking two steps ahead of everyone else.

An advertising and marketing executive found a very creative way to break through the clutter. This woman is known and appreciated for her wit, her stylish appearance, and her reckoning of a client's state of mind. Once, when pitching a new account to the chairman of the board—who she knew was a real stuffy financial type—she opened the dialogue by saying, "Excuse me, sir. Do you sleep in the nude?" The chairman almost fell out of his chair. And she got the business.

At the Agency we constantly come up with things that are a creative step above. For example, we once handled a young actor who was pretty much just starting out in the business. Our public relations campaign focused not only on getting him mentioned in the press, but also on making sure he was "seen"—simply getting him "out there." During our campaign, Oprah Winfrey was doing a special show about mothers picking the ideal man for their daughters, and we managed to have our client selected as one of the twenty bachelors who would appear on the program. We knew, of course, that merely getting him on the show was great in itself. *Oprah*, after all, is one of the highest-rated shows on television. Millions would see our client and be made aware of who he was and what he was doing in his career.

But I also knew that because he was going to be among a group of twenty young, good-looking hunks, my client would have to do something to garner extra attention. The show was set up so that the bachelors would all be seated on stage and the mothers would come out with their daughters to be introduced to their "ideal man." What to do so that our client would stand out? Sure, we could have had him do something outrageous, which, although it might have grabbed attention, might not have been appropriate or very cool. Rather, we opted for something simple yet classy. Our client brought flowers for the mother—since she had selected him—and a small, inexpensive gift for her daughter. When he was introduced, he presented his offerings and immediately struck a chord with the mother and the daughter, as well as with the studio audience and even Oprah herself. Not one of the other guys thought to do something like that, and our client stood out as a thoughtful and considerate gentleman. Everyone on the set commented positively about this simple gesture. (Except, of course, the nineteen other guys, who were busy kicking themselves for not thinking ahead.) Our client received accolades for months afterward from people who had seen the show—fans, industry folks, his peers. You can't buy attention like that.

The public relations business, like any type of business, presents many challenges and obstacles. But I don't know the meaning of the word *can't.* We at the Agency don't give up. And rarely do we take no for an answer. What we try to do is blend persistence with creativity to reach our goals and objectives.

I remember the time I had tried reaching out to a reporter at one of the daily newspapers in New York to pitch him about a client. No less than fifteen phone calls were made—all without a response. We sent letters, notes, singing telegrams. (Well, maybe not telegrams, but we tried *everything* else!) The result? Nothing. Nada. I was frustrated, and it began really eating away at me.

I happened to be in a gift store picking up cards when I noticed the Halloween decorations over in the corner. One particular item caught my eye: those rubber skeletons that hang from doorways and ceilings. I bought a bunch of them and immediately sent one off to the reporter with a note that said something like: "See what I've become? Wasting away waiting for your phone call."

That finally did the trick, and I heard from the guy the next day. We have since developed a strong working relationship.

You can be creative by taking the time to know the person you're trying to contact or deal with—even those with whom you've already established a relationship. And remember, the support staff or friends of the person can help you. A college student once sent me a gift I'll never forget. In my business you often find yourself doing favors for people, and they usually reciprocate in one way or another. Often I'm sent an arrangement of flowers—which, as I said before, is nice but doesn't require a hell of a lot of thought. Know what I'm saying? So one day when a long, narrow box—the kind of container in which you'll usually find roses—arrived from the student, I figured, Here we go again. Much to my surprise and delight, however, I opened the box and found three bags of my favorite potato chips. The gesture made me stop and smile. This guy cared enough and took the time to check with my assistant as to what might be a nice but inexpensive gift that would be memorable. It was a little thing, but it made a big difference.

We see numerous innovations every day—in our personal lives, in business, and in the consumer market—that are great examples of "going the extra mile" by combining persistence, creativity, and a knowledge of people in the targeted market. The Japanese have long stood out as innovators. And I often think of a couple of examples that may seem like small things but, when you really think about it, speak volumes for their creativity. Everyone knows the sheer joy of eating an ice-cream cone on a hot summer day—or even on a cold winter day if you're really into ice cream. But the ice cream eventually starts melting and then begins dripping out the bottom of the cone. Makes for quite a mess, right? Well, a friend and former client, Triloka recording artist/jazz musician Rene McLean, was over in Tokyo on tour and came back with a great story. He said that when he got an ice-cream cone he noticed that the Japanese had come up with the brilliant idea of putting a small ball of candy in the bottom of the cone. It stopped the drips *and* you got an extra treat at the end. A small gesture, to be sure. But the simplistic creativity behind the idea is pure genius! I love it.

The Japanese have long been known for their dedicated and persistent work ethic, and that's the simple explanation as to why their electronics, cars, and other manufactured equipment stand out as some of the best in the industrialized world. The buzz word in Japanese business practices has always been "quality," and their ideas—from microchips to ice-cream cones—have always reflected creative thinking and "finding a way." Another example of a creative thing that speaks volumes for the Japanese inventive ways: Hail a cab in Tokyo, and as the car pulls up to you the driver presses a button inside the cab and the doors open automatically for you. Great!

I recently heard about another innovative way to get something done. Have you ever been nabbed for a speeding ticket or two? Or maybe you've had some other driving infractions and the Department of Motor Vehicles says you have to go "back to school." Well, in Los Angeles, offenders who must take driving classes again are surprised to find out that the DMV has hired comedians to help teach their classes. Of course, driving safely is a serious matter. But in Los Angeles they have realized that comedy can be a useful learning tool because people are apt to retain and learn more if they are in a more relaxed atmosphere. A little creativity goes a long way.

Chapter 22

Finding a Way

To consistently stand out and succeed, you need to be able to *find a way*. Whatever needs doing, find a way to do it. Nothing is impossible (though the improbable may take a little longer). To find a way, you need to acquire (or hone) skills in two key areas, persistence and creativity. Finding a way will always enhance your image, improve your reputation, and ultimately lead you to a more productive and successful life.

Finding a way to make a difference and succeed also sometimes means taking a chance. Take a risk. And if you feel that knot in your stomach, you know it's risk time, so go with it! It means you are on the right track to great things. Think about it: anytime you ever started anything new or distinctive, you had that knot in your stomach, didn't you? It's human nature to be apprehensive about new things. But go ahead and find a way to be different, be bold, be daring.

Arsenio Hall certainly took a chance. When he first

started his late night show critics were skeptical of this young, hip talk show host. Even his guests were different—where else could you find ninety-year-old comedian George Burns on the same show with controversial rapper Ice-T? But, of course, Arsenio proved them all wrong, taking hold and establishing his show against the stiffest competition, where many others had failed.

Remember earlier when I said that changing careers was a bold move for me? If you want to talk "bold," take an example from actress Sheryl Lee Ralph, one of the original cast members of Broadway's *Dreamgirls*. Before the last presidential election, Ralph was hosting a campaign fundraiser for Bill Clinton when someone arrived whom Ralph didn't know but thought "had vibes." She went up to introduce herself to the man, who turned out to be Harry Thomason, an "FOB" ("Friend of Bill" Clinton) and executive producer of the television show *Designing Women*. After their introduction, Ralph grabbed him by his lapels and said—right in his face—"After seven years, I cannot believe you can't find a Black woman to befriend those women in Atlanta."

Thomason was obviously taken aback and replied, "Who are you?!" Sheryl Lee, clearly on a roll, shoots right back with, "I'm Sheryl Lee Ralph, and I should be on your show." (You go, girl!) Two months later Sheryl Lee was a regular on the program.

Talk about finding a way!

Or how about the woman who runs her own catering service in Manhattan and who finds a way to reach prospective customers by walking into Wall Street's trading rooms—unannounced—at lunchtime because people are in a more receptive mood at that time? She knows that once she gets her food samples into people's mouths, she'll have more clients. So four days a week she fills a basket with food and fliers and takes the subway downtown.

If you are selling a product or are in the business of servicing people or companies, you'll always need to find a way to reach more customers. A few chapters back I mentioned that a company had apologized by sending elaborate stand-up cutouts to a client. The firm, J&M Advertising (in Los Angeles), found another way to use those cartoonish cutouts. Sam Johnson, the president of the company, had special ones made up in an effort to secure new business. He had a plan to send out three of them—once a week—to people he wanted to bring in as clients. The three cutouts were in stages, illustrating the incredible pressure of the advertising business, and they were pretty outlandish. The first one depicted a stressed-out client with his brain literally flying out of his head; the second one had the figure smashing his brain on the desk to get the "creative juices" flowing; and the third and final one had the guy in a straitjacket (with his brain—thankfully—back in place). The copy accompanying the cutout read "Now you have time to call a professional."

As I said, pretty bizarre. But very creative. And it worked. The first person to call Johnson was Michael King of King World Entertainment—an incredibly powerful businessman who immediately noticed, and was impressed by, the creativity. Other successful people—accomplished in their own terms of creativity—also were struck by the process of the creative input, understood it, appreciated it, and called Johnson themselves. Business eventually tripled, Johnson said, from sending out those things.

As mentioned earlier, a little thing like saying "Thank you" goes a long way toward succeeding. Finding a way to say thanks and, better yet, knowing how to show your appreciation in various business settings will always be noticed. There was an instance where a reporter had written a great feature story on me and the Agency, and I of course wanted to show my gratitude. I sent a nice letter, along with a small package of decorative notecards, as a gesture of my thanks. The reporter returned the gift, however, telling me that it was against company policy to accept the favor. She then pointed out that the most she could accept was a cup of coffee. We both knew that our hectic schedules probably wouldn't allow even that to happen, but I couldn't let it drop at that. It took me over a month to find, but I finally came across one of those "spilled coffee cup" gags, and I sent that along to her with a note that read "Guess I shouldn't have tried to mail the coffee. . . ." Her company policy wasn't violated, and the thanks was given in a way that will surely be remembered.

In today's world, you will certainly succeed by applying all the personal touch methods I'm describing in this book. Another important vehicle needed on the road to success, however, is a way to market yourself. Nothing is more personal: toot your own horn. Let people know what you're doing. Share your work and yourself with others. And by finding a creative way to let the world know what you're all about, you will get to the top. Let me give you some examples.

Oscar Micheaux, one of the first Black filmmakers, was a feverishly aggressive entrepreneur and marketing specialist. A prolific novelist and moviemaker, Micheaux traveled by car all across the country, hawking his wares. He would sell his books or try to line up screenings for his movies from the back of his car. He would meet with leaders of the Black communities—doctors, lawyers, and businessmen—as well as with Black laborers, domestics, and farmers. He would lecture in schools, in churches, even in homes, promoting himself and his work. His name quickly circulated through the Black community, and he eventually acquired quite a following.

Spike Lee is also a wizard at marketing. Tireless in his campaigns, he takes the art of self-promotion to an unprecedented level. His actions, commentary, and film subject matter are often deemed controversial by the media and industry insiders, so he gets a lot of play. Spike uses the press expertly. I know I don't have to tell you that Spike is one of the most talked about directors of his day—thanks in large part, I'm sure, to his talent for marketing.

Alan Stillman, head of the New York Restaurant Group, often talks about the importance of promoting himself and his group. "I 'public relate,' " he said in a *Crain's New York Business* article, coining a verb. "I have to public relate, because if people don't know what you are, you're nothing." Stillman's own iconoclastic brand of aggressive marketing helped NYRG grow even through the early 1990s, one of the toughest economic climates the restaurant industry has ever seen. People do indeed know Stillman. They know his group.

Marketing one's self and one's company is an ongoing, everyday, think-about-it-all-the-time duty. It doesn't matter where you are or what you're doing. . . .

I was once in a cab and the driver asked me if I'd like to read some of his poetry. I really didn't, but I said okay. I skimmed it and said that I liked what I read. So then he tells me that he has copies of his latest book of poems. Here's a cabdriver, smack in the middle of New York City rush hour, marketing himself and his book. I gotta say, I smiled. I was impressed, and I certainly appreciated his entrepreneurial spirit. So, of course, I bought one of his books.

I'm always "public relating" an event, a new film, a new album, anything that we're working on or handling. I'll leave fliers announcing an event in the back of taxicabs, on buses, in doctor's offices, at airports, everywhere I go. You gotta find a way. And every time I call attention to a project or client, I'm marketing The TWA at the same time. Which will lead to more business. Which will lead to greater success.

Chapter 23

The Extras

Ron Meyer is president of Creative Artists Agency, widely considered the most powerful talent agency in Hollywood. Meyer personally handles some of the biggest stars in entertainment, including Michael Douglas, Whoopi Goldberg, and Tom Cruise. And although Meyer is not as well known or as visible as his partner, CAA chairman Mike Ovitz, he is known and respected as "the power behind the power." In a *Wall Street Journal* article profiling the superagent, it was pointed out that Meyer is also known for "going the extra mile for his clients." When Sylvester Stallone was filming *Cliffhanger,* the movie was running over budget and Stallone was forced to put up $750,000 of his own to shoot a difficult stunt scene. Ron Meyer also put in over $100,000 of his own money to help out. In the dog-eat-dog world of Hollywood, it is—to say the least—quite unusual for an agent to give money rather than take it.

Ron Meyer earns respect, loyalty, and success (and, of

course, a hell of a lot of money) by doing that unexpected "extra" for his company and his clients. A sure way to stand out is to go a little beyond the ordinary. If you think you've handled a task well, sit back and look for what else can be done. There is *always* something extra. It takes a little thought and imagination. Pay attention to the details. Get to know the likes—and dislikes—of the people you're dealing with. What drives them, inspires them, interests them? Any extra action or gesture on your part will mean much more if some thought has been put into it.

Follow the lead of Stan Bromley, general manager of the Four Seasons Hotel in Washington, D.C. To say that Bromley goes that "extra mile" is a supreme understatement. Check into the Four Seasons with your pooch, for example, and good old Fido gets a gift—a bowl filled with doggie biscuits—and even a note from Bromley. Jim Nassikas, who once owned the famed Stanford Court Hotel in San Francisco and is a legend among those in the hotelier trade, once said of Bromley: "Stan is highly sensitive to the monumentally magnificent trivialities—the details—and that makes him great."

When former First Lady Barbara Bush stopped by the hotel for tea, First Dog Millie was presented with a strand of faux pearls that matched her mistress's. In the hotel's fitness club, every StairMaster, treadmill, and stationary bike has its own TV, VCR, and stereo player with remote control and headphones. And while other hotel health spas may provide water or sodas for sale, Bromley supplies fresh-squeezed orange juice, soft drinks, bottled water, coffee, and tea—all at no charge. That's what keeps people coming back.

Steve Ross, the late head of the megaconglomerate Time Warner (which includes the company that publishes this book), consistently went the extra mile. His gestures were often unexpected. Why? Simply because people of his power and stature weren't supposed to call employees and ask about their health and their families. Ross did. The boss of a giant company like Time Warner isn't supposed to notice that a dinner companion particularly enjoyed a certain wine and then send them a whole case of it the next day. Ross did. He took care of the "extra" things, the things that went above and beyond, and those gestures earned him worldwide respect and admiration, not to mention loyalty from employees—and Warner Bros.' stable of stars. When he died in 1993, without fail every story about him mentioned the nice things he did for people. No amount of hard-nosed wheeling and dealing or intellectual prowess alone can earn you such warm regard.

Like Ross, hotelier Bromley pays attention. And he knows his clientele. Ron Galotti, the former publisher of *Vanity Fair* magazine, once said, "Who else would send you a note that says he was offended to learn you stayed in another Washington hotel? How did he even know I was in town?" Galotti says that Bromley "makes you feel special. He cares that you're comfortable."

Caring counts . . . and is another "extra." It's an innate human quality that more of us should exhibit from time to time. Even when you make a mistake—and again, we all make mistakes—if you care about righting the wrong, it can have a positive impact. Bromley says, "We're going to make mistakes, but it's how you handle them that saves you." Once, a guest's prototype package was accidentally thrown out by a room maid at Bromley's hotel. By way of apology, on the guest's next visit Bromley personally met him at the airport in a limousine, had a bag of goodies in the backseat for the guest to munch on, and drove him off to a ball game—something Bromley knew the guest would like—before checking him in at the hotel.

The Ritz-Carlton Hotel chain also maintains a caring, thoughtful philosophy that has made the company world renowned for service and quality. They drum into their employees—in orientation programs, daily inspections, and periodic reviews—the necessity for "going the extra mile." No detail is too small, no request too large. This means giving each guest a warm welcome every day, saying "Good morning" or "Good afternoon." Never "Hi" or "How's it going?" It means escorting guests who ask directions, rather than pointing the way. And it means taking responsibility for a guest's complaint and seeing that it is resolved.

Bob Gutkowski, president and chief executive officer of Madison Square Garden, also embodies the "extra" qualities that have enabled him to succeed: his successful business acumen is proven, and, as he was quoted recently as saying, "My father taught me that you have to deal with people above you and below in the same manner. You have to show respect." Indeed, says one of Gutkowski's co-workers, "From the top brass to the people who mop the floors, he is visible, approachable, and he finds out what's needed."

Another of Gutkowski's special touches: An executive for a computer software firm had spent almost $70 for New York Rangers (ice hockey) tickets as Christmas presents for his son and nephew. He was, understandably, upset when the seats turned out to be in nosebleed territory; they couldn't even see the goal.

"I was furious," the man said. "So I wrote a letter. Most of the time you don't hear anything back or you hear from some flunky. But Gutkowski called me himself. I was shocked. He said I could have three tickets to any other game. [We] went to see the Islanders and sat behind their bench. My son and nephew were thrilled."

You can't begin to measure the goodwill Bob's personal touch gesture generated. I met him once about eight years ago at an NATPE (National Association of Television Program Executives) convention when I was at Essence. Throughout the years I've run into him at the Garden or other events, and though I know he really doesn't know who I am, he vaguely recognizes my face and he's always friendly and gracious. And I appreciate that quality in him. It's the human, personal touch. Most executives and businesspeople say you can't teach it. But I say it *can* be learned. And it *will* make a difference in your personal life, your business, and your dealings with other people.

Bob Gutkowski certainly stood out when he personally called a dissatisfied customer. He could have had his assistant send out a form letter, or he might have simply ignored a fan who was just "bitching and moaning." Instead he imparted a personal touch and made a difference by doing something special.

Like these successful businesspeople, you can learn to succeed by taking the time to know the person you're trying to contact or deal with—even those with whom you've already established a relationship. I did something a little "extra" for a friend who happens to be a well-known entertainer. We met several years ago, established that all-important rapport, and then tried to stay in touch over the years. As she became increasingly involved with her projects and work, I knew it would be difficult to get a response from the notes and letters I sent—let alone from my phone calls. This was certainly understandable. After all, the woman was incredibly busy. But I also knew that I had to find a way to grab her attention. So what I came up with is really quite simple, but it definitely did the trick. I simply send her a postcard, and on the card I wrote: "Just wanted to touch base. . . . Check off where appropriate." And below the written note I had little boxes next to phrases like "I'm fine"; "Things are going well"; "Reeeaaallly busy." The postcard was stamped and addressed to me. All she had to do was take a minute to check off a box or two and my mission was completed. It made her smile—and me stand out.

I even did the same thing for a guy I was interested in a while back. Sent him a card with an invitation to dinner. And below were the boxes next to phrases such as "I'd love to go out with you, Terrie" or "Can't right now, too busy. But please call." It got him. Or I should say, I got him. He checked box number one, and we ended up dating for several months. And we're still friends.

Remember that it's unwise to sit back and rest on your laurels when conducting business. Do the "extra" and always try to cultivate new friendships—which turn into new business—and always, always maintain contact with old clients, current customers, of course, and even prospective accounts. I had special "FYI" cards made up quite a while ago that read "Thought you might find the enclosed of interest." Whenever I come across an article in a magazine or newspaper (or any of the twenty or so publications I read each week) that I think someone (particularly a client) would appreciate seeing, I clip it out, attach one of my cards, and send it along with a short note. You can provide this service, and it shows you care about that person and their interests. This keeps the information flowing, and, more important, it keeps your name in front of people. I'm telling you I've gotten enough positive feedback to know it is appreciated.

Applying the little extras will help you succeed by getting the job done—in a different, creative way. Do that well enough and often enough and people will start to notice. Believe me, people are watching. Case in point: The premiere of the epic Spike Lee movie *Malcolm X* drew press from all over New York. The day of the premiere our office received a ton of calls from press and others who wanted to attend; they thought we were handling the event, even though we weren't. And that's because of our reputation in handling other films. The next day we got a call from a local paper, which wanted to print a photograph of Malcolm's widow, Betty Shabazz, and four of her six daughters. The people at the paper needed help in identifying the girls. They had tried the film's distributor but had not gotten a call back. (In all fairness to the film company, maybe they didn't get the message—it does happen.) So the people at the paper called us. Why? Because even though we weren't working on the film, or the premiere, or even with Spike or any of the Shabazz women, they just knew that we would at least take the time to assist them. And, of course, we did.

Remember the Friars Club roast where Ted Danson appeared in blackface to "honor" Whoopi Goldberg? Montel Williams, as you may recall, was incredibly upset by the whole show and contacted me right after walking out of the luncheon. He wanted to send apologies to those women of color who were in attendance—and he knew that, even though I had no official involvement with the event or the guests, I could (and would) assist him in reaching those folks.

We often handle film premieres and other events where we have to deal with hordes of media people: photographers, writers, broadcast crews. We know most of them, and most of them know us. Which, sometimes—to be totally honest—can be a real pain in the ass. Because if the press do know you, they feel it is then their privilege or right to ask you to help them out. And then it sometimes becomes "Yo, Terrie, have that star turn this way. . . ." "Hey, Ms. Williams, bring that celebrity over to my camera crew first. . . ." "Aw, shit, Terrie. I missed that shot. Can you get that person out here again?" I've certainly learned that it takes a special kind of candor, and knowledge of the needs of the press, to be able to pull off this stuff without going crazy—especially when the media hounds are barking at you from all different directions.

But it is my job, after all, to make sure the press are accommodated and taken care of at any event we handle. And the Agency is well known for throwing in "extras" on the job.

Eddie Murphy's wedding to the former Nicole Mitchell was the supreme example of going the "extra yard." When we arrived at the Plaza Hotel in New York—where the wedding ceremony and reception were to take place—five hours before the event, over forty newspeople were already lined up outside the door. I had handled three celebrity weddings in the past (baseball star Dave Winfield and Tonya Turner; former New York Knick Mark Jackson and songstress Desiree Coleman; and NBA star John Salley and Natasha Duff), but never one of this magnitude. Accommodating the media is always a challenge, and this event—dubbed "the wedding of the year" by many of the press—certainly proved to be one of the most difficult. Eddie and Nicole, though, did make my job a little easier by deciding before the wedding that *Ebony* magazine would have exclusive photo rights to the ceremony and reception. This eliminated the task of coordinating a photo opportunity for all the press.

However, there were still dozens of photographers, reporters, and camera crews standing outside the entrance to the Plaza to catch the celebrity guests arriving for the wedding. Some of the press, of course, had been waiting for hours. And I knew they were disappointed at not being able to see the new bride and groom because they had given the photo exclusive. And they were all freezing; it was one of the coldest March days I can remember. To try to satisfy the interests of the gathered media, I made sure that each arriving star—from Robert Townsend and Bruce

Willis to Charles Dutton and Heavy D—paused long enough to have his or her picture taken and/or speak with most of the film crews.

To try to appease the press, we brought out Vernon Lynch, Eddie's father, who was staying in the hotel, to meet them. We even had Eddie's young nephew, Charlie, who was the ring bearer, and Eddie's brothers, Charlie and Vernon, pose for photos. The press loved it. Then someone asked to see the wedding invitation. So I called back to our "wedding headquarters" (the office, that is) and asked for the invitation to be brought over. It was, and I showed it to all the press. I even went across the street to the throng of fans and let them have a peek. And for another "extra yard" touch—knowing the members of the press were freezing their asses off—we brought out hot chocolate, coffee, and tea. For days afterward I heard from press people, thanking us and commending us for the way the event was handled.

Believe me, if there were any press people there who didn't know me or the Agency before that night, they do now!

Other ways to go the extra mile can be amazingly simple: little things that we all can do any day, anywhere, anytime. And believe me—like the candy "plug" in an ice-cream cone—these actions can help you succeed on every level. Take note. . . .

When sending someone flowers or a nice exotic arrangement, *always* make sure to put both your first and last names on the card. Never assume that you will be recognized by your first name only—unless you're Arsenio, Cher, or Madonna.

You never know when you may need a birthday, anniversary, or even a sympathy card to send out. Here's a time management tip: Always keep a supply of cards for every occasion—and even some blank ones—in your office or at home. And when sending cards, use ones that are thoughtful, creative, and surprising. They can work for you in a number of ways. Here's one example: When I was at Essence Communications, I sent a very distinctive card (it was black, with gold designs on the cover, and I signed my name in gold ink) to former NBC chief executive officer Grant Tinker, who was going to be honored at an upcoming dinner. I had long admired his style and graciousness from afar, and I said so in the note. I sent it just days before the dinner, where I knew I'd have the opportunity to meet him at the reception beforehand. The night of the event I approached Mr. Tinker and introduced myself. He knew who I was immediately, and his first comments were about the card. This allowed me to meet someone I may not have had the chance to otherwise. That little extra attentiveness reaps many rewards and opens countless doors.

The next time you're invited to a bridal or baby shower, or even to a wedding, go that "extra mile": make one of your gifts a nice, decorative set of "thank you" cards and put stamps on the envelopes for the cards. That way, the person will just have to write out her thanks and send them off, without even having to worry about getting stamps.

When flying—if you're the one at your company who gets to fly first class while co-workers or assistants must fly coach, remember what the film producer Ed Saxon, Oscar Award–winning director Jonathan Demme's partner, does when he finds himself in that situation. Saxon makes sure his people (he says these are the folks who have his back) are taken care of by taking (sneaking) them first-class goodies and drinks. This may annoy the flight attendants—I even once watched him do this and get "yelled" at—so you should try to be as discreet as possible.

If you know you'll be taking the same flight as someone you'd like to meet or impress, try to find a way to sit near the person. That way you can introduce yourself and maybe engage in some productive conversation. (Be careful here, though. Some folks, especially celebrities, do *not* like to be intruded upon.) If you can go that special "extra mile," go for it. For example, at the airport I once ran into the assistant of a major client. Knowing that I wanted to establish a good rapport with her, I used some of my frequent flyer bonuses to have her upgraded to business class. We didn't sit next to each other (I did want my space), but we had a delightful trip with quite a few chances to talk. I learned a lot more about her, her boss, and her other colleagues. And I knew that I had made an impression on her that would not be soon forgotten—she ended up referring a lot of business our way.

Chapter 24

Others' Needs

All that is required for the triumph of evil is that good men remain silent and do nothing.

—Edmund Burke

When you are aware of other people's needs and wants, you have many opportunities to go the extra mile to success . . . *if* you take advantage of them. An example: At Eddie's wedding, rapper/actor Heavy D was accompanied by Nia Long, who had featured roles in the John Singleton movie *Boyz 'N the Hood* and the Whoopi Goldberg/Ted Danson feature *Made in America.*

Although Nia's face looked familiar to the members of the press, I sensed that maybe some of them didn't really know who she was. So as she and Heavy were walking into the hotel, I made sure to yell out her name to the press and to mention the movies she had been in. I really love to share people's accomplishments—it makes them feel good, and they appreciate the acknowledgment. Plus, it provides useful information to whomever I'm talking to (or, in this case, yelling at). The press may not even take a photo of the person I'm yelling about, but at least they know for the future. A few days after the wedding I received a real sweet note from Nia thanking me for looking out for her. That's what makes it all worthwhile.

Wendell Scales, who is a dentist in Detroit, has built a hugely successful practice by understanding the needs of his patients. Everyone has at one time or another been afraid to go to the dentist. So Wendell makes his offices plush and comfortable and geared toward relaxing his patients. Wendell even offers what he calls "phobia therapy" for those who are frightened of the dentist's chair. This counseling not only helps his patients overcome their dental fears, it can help them in their personal and business lives as well. Wendell cares about his patients, and his practice—as his brochure says—"makes a tremendous difference in the life of each person that walks through the door. As a result of the love and excellence that we give, each person will hesitate to leave because they will face a harsher world outside our door. We are unconditionally committed to removing any limitations or obstacles in the way that would prevent us from making this a reality for [our patients]."

A funeral home in Georgia has another way to meet its clients' needs. One of the most heart-wrenching, personally painful duties a person will ever endure is making the funeral arrangements for a loved one or good friend. And while your typical funeral director may certainly be learned in the art of "expressing his condolences," you might agree that there may not be much feeling behind the words. But I'm sure you will agree that when it comes right down to it, it really is just a job. (And in fairness to any funeral directors out there, I also realize that you simply can't get *too* involved—that's too much grief to take upon yourself.)

One Georgia funeral home has found a way to go that extra mile by offering a few added—and unexpected—services by providing small catered receptions (punch and sandwiches) for the bereaved family after the wake or after the funeral at no extra charge. The place cares enough to know that family members have enough on their minds without having to worry about what to serve everyone when they come back to the house.

Or here's another, admittedly odd, variation on the meeting people's needs theme. An innovative funeral parlor owner in Florida found a way to distinguish himself from more established competitors: a drive-by window affording mourners a view of the deceased. He says it appeals to the elderly and the disabled who may have trouble getting in and out of cars. And it also works for those who want to pay respects but don't want to dress up and meet all the relatives. A bit off the wall, for sure. But, hey, you should pay attention to these kinds of examples—no matter how bizarre. You don't have to like or agree with them, but you've got to admire the thought process. And you can't argue with success. This guy's business has moved up to the number two spot in the marketplace.

Another proof-is-in-the-pudding example: I attended an NBA all-star game a few years back and noticed that Richard Lawson, that fine-looking actor of stage, television, and film, had gotten himself literally surrounded by a horde of screaming women, who were asking him to pose for pictures and sign autographs. Richard is very accommodating to his fans and will spend the time—however long it takes—to meet and greet the people who come up to him. On this day, however, I noticed from afar that he seemed a little overwhelmed. The game was about to start, and I could tell that Richard wanted to get to his seat.

Though I'd never met him, I tried to make eye contact with him, and when we did finally look at each other, I mouthed the words "Would you like to get away?" Richard quickly nodded, so I burst forth through the throng and as "Richard's publicist," thanked the women for their interest and gently guided him away (saying Mr. Lawson really needed to get to his seat). He was very thankful, and that began a great friendship and business relationship. We have the pleasure of working with Richard today, and he remains a good friend.

David Stern, the commissioner of the National Basketball Association, has certainly made a difference in his job by the immense success he has had in positioning the NBA as the premier sports entertainment entity. He's also been a friend/mentor to me throughout the years. He will call from time to time just to check up on me or to see if I need anything. I will never forget the time shortly after David and I met that he set up a meeting for me with someone. David knew that I was starting my own business, so he thought I might like the chance to speak with a person in the public relations biz. So I'm thinking: Thank you very much, David, I appreciate it. Then David tells me the meeting is with Howard Rubenstein. Now, Howard Rubenstein is like "Mr. Public Relations" in New York! He handles everyone—there simply is no one else in PR. (Well, now there's me!) And there I was, soon after opening my own firm, sitting with David and a true legend, whom I was able to talk with and ask questions of. It was unreal.

But that's the kind of person David Stern is. When I was to receive the prestigious Matrix Award from New York Women in Communications—quite an honor, I must say, and I was the first African-American woman to receive the award for public relations—I asked David if he would do me the honor of presenting me the plaque at the awards luncheon, which was being held at the Waldorf-Astoria. I was aware of David's hectic schedule and, therefore, promised him it wouldn't take more than a half hour of his time. You can imagine my horror when the thing went on, and on, and on, and three and a half hours later David is finally handing me my award. But he graciously endured the wait and made me one of the proudest—and most thankful—recipients there that day. (I'm sure the other winners from that year, and their presenters, including Joan Lunden, Annie Leibovitz, Grace Mirabella, Peter Jennings, and Carol Channing, were also very proud—and behind schedule—that day.)

Even a little gesture on someone's part—given with the other person's needs in mind—can have a major impact on your life and make a difference. Enid Nemy, the fine "Style" writer for *The New York Times,* once taught me a valuable lesson with just one small gesture. When I was first starting out, I had reached out to Enid with a story idea. We became friendly and started to chat on the phone (even if it didn't involve work). She knew I was just breaking into the business. Once she invited me to her annual holiday party. I graciously accepted, and I'll have to admit that when I went to the party I felt, at first, a little weird. I was the only Black person there at that time, and as I scoped out the room I noticed that it was a gathering of "everyone who's anyone" in New York. Enid treated me as one of the gang and never gave the impression that I was out of place. She only felt, I'm sure, that it would be beneficial for me—a young upstart—to start mingling among the who's who. It said a lot about her to reach out to a "nobody" like me. Not many people do that sort of thing—it's very rare.

A few years ago I was backstage at the United Negro College Fund tribute to the legendary Sammy Davis Jr. It had been a rough trip out to Los Angeles, and—as usual—

I had a thousand things on my mind. I remember just kind of standing there in a tension-induced haze, with a frown on my face. Suddenly Bill Cosby came up from behind me and—well, let's just say he "startled" me—and then took off before I could say anything. Of course, I was shocked, but I also couldn't stop laughing. He certainly got me out of my fog. A few days later he called me from the road to explain his actions. "You looked very tense," said the "father" of all comedians. "We need you out here, and I just wanted to tell you that you need to take time out for Terrie. Take that long, luxurious bath, or whatever."

That small gesture made one hell of a big difference for me at that time because Cos was sincerely thinking of me.

David Groh, the actor who played Valerie Harper's boyfriend on *Rhoda,* showed that he is unselfish and thinks of others when he starred in the short-lived Broadway play *Twilight of the Golds* about a year ago. At the time, we were handling Judith Scarpone, a talented actress who co-starred in the play. Although the show got mixed reviews, Judith was praised and received rave comments. The press, however, would usually want to speak with David because he was a bigger "name." Judith pointed out, though, that whenever he was being interviewed David would make sure to mention Judith's name and even tried to see that she was in the room. You don't hear about many actors giving their co-stars their props. David showed that he was a caring, thoughtful, respectful human being.

Director Alan Gansberg has long been a source of support. He often surprises me with little letters of encouragement and sound advice. They're a surprise because I never know when to expect them, and these warm notes are not necessarily sent "because" of a certain event, situation, or circumstance. Alan just comes through for me because he recognizes my needs. I once mentioned to him during a hurried phone call that I'd rather have things in writing, because sometimes there simply is too much verbal input during the day. A few weeks later I received a note that read "I have enclosed some ready-to-use notes and reminders. Glad to be of service." It was wonderful! The notes were just nice little things like "Take time for yourself," and they made my day because they were offered in a purely unselfish manner. When taking care of others' needs, I hope that you are giving of yourself "because you want to." As an added incentive, though, think of yourself or others who are dear to you being caught in various situations. I was once driving home and saw an elderly woman waiting for a bus. It was a terribly cold night, and it was pretty late. All I could think of was my grandmother and how she would feel waiting in the dark, alone—and I couldn't handle that image. I was mortified. I pulled over and went up to the woman, saying: "I know you might think this is a little weird—this being New York and all—but I was wondering if I could give you a ride somewhere." She was a bit startled, but she did finally realize that I wasn't a threat and allowed me to drive her home. So it took me an extra twenty minutes—it helped make an elderly lady a little safer and warmer.

Many businesses today are even responding to the needs of their customers and their employees by providing services that were unheard of a few years ago. As an example: One of the fastest-growing professions out there is the "corporate concierge." We're all familiar with the concierge behind the lobby desk of a hotel—that friendly person who can direct you to a certain restaurant in town or take care of your dry cleaning. The corporate concierge acts basically on the same premise: he or she is there to help the employees of a business take care of personal chores. Probably one of the first companies to do this was PepsiCo, which employed a gentleman to mind other workers' personal business so they can keep their minds on their work. This worker's worker, so to speak, will have your car's oil changed, get your suit tailored, make the anniversary dinner reservations, or provide that night's theater tickets. PepsiCo started this unique employee benefit perk a couple of years ago after a companywide survey showed that workers were stressed out because they didn't have the time to take care of their personal errands. Employing the services of the concierge has increased productivity at the company, decreased absenteeism, and, as one of PepsiCo's employee services managers stated, "ensured that we remain an employer of choice." Many other companies have now followed the lead of PepsiCo in supplying their employees with a professional "go-fer."

Another business that is providing for the needs of today's customers is the hotel industry. As we saw earlier, the nicer hotels such as the Ritz-Carlton and the Four Seasons certainly know how to accommodate their guests. But now even midpriced hotels are going that extra mile. Places that used to offer only HBO or Cinemax as added amenities are now equipping guest rooms with fax machines, computers, and larger desks, thereby creating a kind of mini-office away from the office. As one manager said, "You would lose many more guests looking to use this room by not having computers. You have to have full service or no service at all." Many hotels are now providing extra phone lines, modem hookups for computers, and in-room coffee makers.

And on the personal touch, here are some other hotel incentives designed to attract guests: the use of a Sega video game for the kids (and the grown-ups!), offered by Howard Johnson's and included in the price of the room; a disposable camera for families, provided by participating Ramada Inns; and—this one supplied by some smaller hotels in the midwest to offer guests a little touch of home—a free cat for the night, complete with a fresh supply of kitty food and litter.

I was once waiting at a hotel check-out desk and had put my two heavy bags on the floor as I was waiting for the clerk to finish her paperwork. It looked as though she were almost ready, so I picked up my bags again and put them on my shoulder. Yet it was still a few more seconds, and the woman noticed that and said, "I'm sorry you had to wait a little while longer." She was observant and sensitive to my needs and the situation. It was a little thing that meant a lot. Just as if you're coming out of your apartment and see someone heading up the walk laden with packages, take a second and hold the door open. It won't take a minute of your time, and you've helped someone in a difficult situation. Similarly, when you're on a plane, take the time to notice if you can help anybody with their bags, stowing them or taking them down from the overhead compartment.

And don't forget those who may be less fortunate than you. Those of us who live in cities—with their ever-growing population of homeless, beggars, and panhandlers—are confronted almost daily by people asking for money. Maybe you feel that your donated money will just be spent on drugs or alcohol, or maybe you feel a little guilty by not contributing at all. Here's something you can do to meet their immediate needs: When you're out at a restaurant and there are some leftovers, ask for a doggie bag. Then go that extra yard for a fellow human and put the food outside on top of a trash can or mailbox—homeless people often get their meals that way. In fact, I got the idea from a television movie that starred Lucille Ball as a homeless woman, and she was teaching a newly homeless person how to fend for herself by searching through trash cans. I try to share my food this way all the time (that is, if

I don't take the food home for myself). Try it sometime—you'll like the feeling of knowing that you've helped someone. It will reflect positively on you and on the people you are dealing with. And it will help you succeed.

When you do something for someone else, you end up doing for yourself. I mentioned airlines earlier: think about the part of the flight attendants' safety speech when they tell you that in case of a loss of cabin pressure, you should put your oxygen masks on first, then help children or others who might need assistance. That's a nice point and a very important lesson. Take care of yourself and you'll be able to assist others. As Susan Taylor at Essence says, "You can't give from an empty cup."

Chapter 25

Standing Out When Starting Out (or Over)

I know from experience how heavy the baggage of anxiety and uncertainty can be when a decision is made to start a career or change professions. But I've acquired the tools that can lighten the load. I've worked with and talked to enough young people and executives in a variety of businesses to know what will make the difference and enable folks to move forward.

When venturing into new or uncharted territories—the killing fields known as the job market—remember:

It's never too early—or too late—to start standing out. A while back *The Wall Street Journal* ran a story about young people preparing for careers in politics. There's a summer course called "Candidate Career Development School," given each year by the Leadership Institute in Springfield, Virginia, which grooms young people for public-policy careers. This truly amazed me. The story quoted a kid who was fourteen—fourteen?!—saying, "I feel I can make a difference." He attended the course because he plans to run for the House or Senate and then the White House. Fourteen! Geezus . . .

The course offers sound advice to these energetic and driven youngsters. And we can all pay attention to the recommendations put forth: The best thing you can do is compile a list of friends. There's an art to making an impression. Send letters to every new person you meet, just to say it was a pleasure to make their acquaintance. Keep records of your contacts. (I know this was mentioned earlier, but I can never stress this enough.) Another lesson that can never be learned too early (or too late): Clean living and righteous thinking always stand out. Avoid the pitfalls of having skeletons in the closet. *You never know* . . . when something will come back to haunt you.

Is it ever too late to start out or start over? No way. Just ask my mother. This incredible woman started college in her fifties (after my sister and I finished high school), then went on to earn her master's degree, and today remains a widely respected force in the Mount Vernon community for her years of commitment, especially because of her work with the PTA. Susan Taylor, the elegant *Essence* editor, also went back in her later years to earn a degree. In fact, after having been in the editor's chair at *Essence* for quite a while, Susan felt a little "inadequate" without a diploma. So after years of being on the job, and single-handedly raising her daughter, Susan adhered to the old adage "Better late than never" and went on to graduate from Fordham University.

When starting out or starting over, you need to be aware of a number of things that will enable you to stand out and raise your chances of getting that new job, or put you at the head of the line for that promotion, or prepare you as you embark on that new career.

Say you find yourself three years into the job and you realize there's no room for advancement and you don't feel there are any other opportunities at the company. Or maybe you've been in the same place for ten years or so and feel that you've got the career doldrums. Perhaps you've recently been laid off or you are just out of college. Whatever the case, it's time to get your résumé—the single most important document you put in front of a prospective employer—in shape. Remember these cardinal rules when preparing or updating your résumé.

- Make sure the document is error free. Mistakes in grammar or spelling are sure ways to get your résumé—and maybe even your career—tossed right into the old "round file." Know what I'm saying?
- Avoid convoluted sentence structure or phrases. Be concise and to the point, and—while you certainly want to highlight special skills or achievements—stay away from glossing it up too much. Saying you were a "petroleum distribution engineer" (read: pumped gas at the local service station) won't fool many employers.
- Be aware that the style of writing résumés has changed over the last few years. Keep up with the latest. Omit photos, salary requirements, reasons for leaving last job, and hobbies (unless they may be related to the profession).
- Never fax your résumé to an executive unless you have been requested to do so. Always mail it in a properly addressed, clean envelope.

Of course, your résumé must be accompanied by a cover letter. Cover letters should be in a standard business format and should never be longer than three paragraphs. Find out to whom the cover letter should be addressed: don't settle for "Personnel Director" or "Dear Sir/Madam."

You'll want to begin your letter by stating the position you are applying for and citing where or how you found out about the job opening. Then you will want to toot your own horn by highlighting your experience and the skills that would enable you to fulfill the requirements of the position. If the shoe fits, elaborate on one or two special accomplishments that strengthen the fact that you're qualified for the job. Finish by communicating a genuine interest and enthusiasm (without going overboard—remember: a load of BS is always apparent) for the job and the company.

And always, always, always, check for spelling, punctuation, grammar. When I receive cover letters that are marred by typos or other mistakes, it's a major turnoff. How could someone expect me seriously to consider them for a job when they haven't even taken the time to construct a professional letter?

Ideally your résumé and cover letter will entice the employer to call you in for an interview, which will be the final test for you. So take note:

The vice president of an outplacement counseling company gets really hot under the collar when people who come in for interviews walk into his office and sit down without asking where he'd like them to sit. "I've actually had people sit on my chair, and they had to walk around my desk to do so!" he fumes.

The president of an executive recruiting firm gets bothered when an interviewee starts scratching her panty hose or whatever else itches. "I'm also annoyed when people check their watch constantly or drum their fingers on the desk. It indicates they have something else on their mind."

These two executives cite examples that—believe it, or not—occur with frightening regularity. Many job applicants—whether it be the still-wet-behind-the-ears graduate or the established professional who has become the latest recession casualty of widespread "staff reorganization"—fall into a number of interview traps that quickly put them at a disadvantage when interviewing for a job. When looking for a new position in the business world, what can you do that will make you stand out among the fifteen other applicants who possess the same education, experience, and knowledge that you do?

You must find a way to break through the clutter and distinguish yourself as a person who not only exhibits all the necessities for the job, but is willing to show that extra initiative. How can you weed through the process and get to the head of the line? Well, now that you asked . . .

Do your homework. Find out as much as you can about the company. Go to the library. Talk to the employees. Even chat with a competitor. Taking the time to do some research will automatically put you ahead of those with whom you may be competing. Statistics show that only 2 percent of potential employees go the extra yard and learn something about the company they are applying with. Do your own "informational interview" by being prepared with a few questions of your own. Asking thought-provoking questions about the position or showing an interest in how a company would handle various situations shows enthusiasm.

Stop, look, and listen. And no, we're not crossing railroad tracks here. You're trying to grab an edge somehow. Listen to what the interviewer says during the conversation. Perhaps he'll mention an upcoming event, project, or even a special birthday or anniversary. Notice what decorates the walls and shelves. Plaques, photographs, awards, and the like will give you an idea as to what the person is involved with. Remember to mention in your follow-up note the event or a relevant piece of information that was brought up or observed. And to really blow someone away? Say the interviewer does mention that his twentieth year with the company will be celebrated next month. Very nonchalantly, say something like "Oh, that's great. What date is that?" Make a mental note—don't noticeably write it down. Then send a congrats card or note that will arrive on the appropriate day. Guaranteed to make you stand out.

Another important point: Once the interview is over, most job applicants assume the rest is up to the employer. Not! Never forget to send a follow-up letter. This is the perfect opportunity to mention that personal fact you heard about or some other topic that was brought up in the interview, or to add something that slipped your mind. Thank the interviewer for meeting with you and take the chance to make one last push for yourself. Embellish on the fact that you are the only one for the job by highlighting an achievement, or relevant skills, or experience that may not have been discussed in the interview. This often overlooked gesture just might provide the edge you need to get the job.

Even when filling out an application, you can bring things to a more personal level. An example: When it comes time for me to fill in my height/weight, I do put down my weight, but then I'll draw a sad face next to it. It always makes the person reading the form smile a bit.

For those of you in the position of interviewer, take note:

Get the applicant to relax before you begin. Start off the conversation with some idle chatter or ask them about their hobbies. Then lead into the interview by talking about your company, and share the job's performance requirements with the candidate.

Phrase questions to avoid an intimidation factor. Instead of "What are your strengths and weaknesses?" try "What do you like to do most?" You want the candidates to open up. And when they do start talking, listen attentively. Interviewees' questions, as well as their answers, will tell you a lot about them.

Although you must be aware of discriminatory queries about religion, marital status, or child care arrangements, I always like to delve a little bit into the person. What does she like to do for fun? What kinds of things does he read? Try to find out something about the *person,* the human side. It's not only a way to get the person in a conversational mood, it will give you some more insight. And don't forget that you, too, must leave a good impression. The best candidates are undoubtedly looking at other options. Make sure that they leave wanting to work for you and your company.

When you get that job—or switch to another company or profession—be aware that the employee rosters of many businesses today are made up of people from diverse races and cultures. Be aware of stereotyping and the resulting foot-in-mouth disease that comes with such ignorance. I certainly wouldn't want a White person coming to a business meeting with me and trying to talk "Black" by saying something like "Yo, sistah, what's happening?" Doesn't cut it, know what I mean? Sometimes the error is harmless, like the time during a staff meeting at the Agency a White staffer consistently referred to the AME Zion church as "African Methodist Episcopal." I laughed and informed her that Black folks never say "African Methodist Episcopal," we just say "AME Zion." Another White person on our team, Susan Nowak, who has helped us build and establish our film department, and who is funny, smart, sensitive, and enlightened, was conducting press interviews at a CEBA (Communications Excellence to Black Audiences) Awards dinner a couple of years ago, and she was saying that she had to get the "African-American filmmakers" who were present (and who were being specially honored that night) to the press room. Once again, I laughed and had to say, "Look around you, Nowak. *All* the filmmakers are African American." The point is, be aware of, and know as much as possible about, the people you are working or dealing with. It should also go without saying that sexist/racist or ethnic slurs, jokes, and actions are always totally unacceptable (everywhere, but especially in the workplace). Unfortunately, for some people this still bears repeating.

If you are still pursuing your education, it's important to realize that your classmates are your competition. Even if you're still in high school, you must realize that good grades aren't enough. Astronomical SAT scores will help, but they're not guaranteed to get you into the college of your choice. You must start early on a path that will enable you to stand out.

The same applies for those looking to alter their career paths or those heading out into the "real world" for the first time. You may have the same skills, experience, and talents that fifty or one hundred other people in your field possess. Something has to give you that edge and help you succeed. Let's take a look at some suggestions.

Be persistent and never quit. We saw earlier the advantages of persistence—so don't let a rejection get you down. If at first you don't succeed . . . don't worry about it. And remember the Boy Scout motto: Be prepared. You will succeed and excel at any task—including a job search—if you approach the assignment well prepared. The Japanese teach their workers that to accomplish the desired results in a competitive market, they must first work hard preparing to do it right the first time. Their motto is "Ready, aim, aim, aim, aim . . . *Fire!*"

Look for ways to proclaim—and enhance—your marketability. Always be willing to toot your own horn (if, that is, it's tootable. You walk a fine line here—so you must honestly evaluate yourself). Get active in a trade or industry association or seminars where you will be able to meet people and, more important, they'll meet you. You've got to set the stage for letting people know who you are and what you do. Go to events—and don't be afraid to go alone. I've often been able to get into certain venues or events simply because I am alone (one more person isn't going to overcrowd any place).

Evaluate your strengths and weaknesses. Focus on activities that interest you and relate to your best qualities. Exceptional intelligence alone doesn't guarantee exceptional achievements. Higher achievers distinguish themselves by matching their skills with appropriate projects.

It's never too late or too early to start heading down the path to success. And although our youth today are faced with enormous pressures and problems—and I'll talk about our future in an upcoming chapter—take heart and know that not all high school and college kids are just into themselves, their cars, their radios, or their Friday night dates. Check out the hundred or so students from Santa Monica College in California who will be working each summer doing community service. These outstanding young people are paired with local community organizations—from homeless shelters to inner-city sports programs—and will get a firsthand opportunity to build civic pride. As one student said: "I look at it as a way of paying back my community. It helps me become a well-rounded person as well and to understand the problems that occur in the community."

Talk about people who are "starting out" on the path to success!

Section Four

Returning

Chapter 26

Success Is Fleeting

Be kind and generous in times of prosperity, so when adversity comes you can bear it.

—African proverb

Once you reach a certain level of success, you must pass it on, find a way to give something back. Success and achievement mean nothing if you get there and don't bring someone along. The fact of the matter is, a lot of people won't (or don't) care how successful you are, unless you stand up for more than your own personal career and ambitions. If you live only for yourself, it will unfortunately matter only to you when you're gone. Make sure that your life means something.

And when you get to the top, know also that nobody is on top forever. Therefore, remember that how you will be treated and regarded when the lights go down will be based on how you treated folks when you were on top. Success *can* be fleeting. It could be gone tomorrow.

I have on my wall at the office an old adage that I heard from comedian Alan King about the four stages of an actor's career. I had it personalized, and I often take a look at it to remind myself that I have to work constantly at my craft. Nothing is forever. It goes like this:

- Who is Terrie Williams?
- Get me Terrie Williams!
- Get me a Terrie Williams clone.
- Who is Terrie Williams?

Think about it.

Do you remember Kathleen Sullivan? This attractive and brainy newswoman burst onto the television scene back in 1984, covering the Winter Olympic Games for ABC. She was an instant hit and made quite a reputation for herself. Three years later she switched over to CBS and became a host of *CBS This Morning*. She was at the top of her broadcasting career. Then stories began to circulate that Sullivan was temperamental and that her capabilities were faltering. She was replaced by Paula Zahn in 1990. Then she disappeared for almost three years. When she showed up again on network television, it was as the pitch woman for a weight-loss program.

Of the three-year forced absence, Sullivan said in a *New York Times* article, "I thought everyone just forgot about me." She said there were times she was barely supporting herself and lost a small fortune on a house she was building. She went through a divorce, and her father died.

People she used to work with—and be friendly with—shunned her. And she learned a brutal lesson about success.

But the lesson was learned, she says. "I have a better sense now that everything could come to an end tomorrow. I found out that our values can get out of whack, thinking all that stuff (money, fame) could make us happy."

Remember that. And as Reverend Al Sharpton pointedly admonishes, "When it's your day, remember that what you're going to be judged on is not the success you've achieved, or how bright you are, but by how many other people's lives your brightness has lit up." Sharpton also commented once—in a brutally honest but totally human admission—that he found it difficult to preside over the funeral of someone who was "just wasting space . . . one who had done nothing productive with his or her life."

Will that person you see in the mirror be someone you can live with?

> *So many of us define ourselves by what we have, what we wear, what kind of house we live in, and what kind of car we drive. If you think of yourself as the woman in the Cartier watch and the Hermès scarf, a house fire will destroy not only your possessions, but your self.*
>
> —LINDA HENLEY, AMERICAN WRITER

Think about that, too. When your time is up, how would you like to be remembered? What kind of legacy do you want to leave behind? That of a person who cared for nothing but material wealth and possessions or of one who made a difference—or at least tried to?

I know what I want. And as I've said a million times before, because so many people have provided me with support, encouragement, and inspiration throughout the years, I'm aware that I will never be able to pay back every debt. As I've also said a million times, everything that goes around, comes around. Nobody stays on top forever.

But, I also know that I can make a dent in what I owe and be generous in my times of prosperity, by committing myself to helping others. And I remind myself every day that it is my calling, my mission, to give of myself—or whatever I can—to those who will follow me. And I know that if I get there before you do, I'm obligated to bore a hole and pull you through.

Chapter 27

To Whom Much Is Given, Much Is Required

I hope this book will help you become a better success and a better person—in your job, in your life, in whatever you do. And I honestly wish you every achievement possible.

But I also hope that once you get there, you'll remember the following quote from Scripture:

To whom much is given, much is required.

Leigh Steinberg is one of the most successful sports agents in the country. He's in a profession that does not regularly receive high accolades. Or, as *Los Angeles Times* sports columnist Scott Ostler put it: "When you're talking about sports agents, a compliment might be something like 'He's not in jail' or 'Some of his clients have decided not to sue him.' "

As I said, not a very good rep. But Leigh Steinberg is doing his own little thing to enhance the lives of his clients—top players in the National Football League, National Basketball Association, and other sports arenas—and, more important, other disadvantaged people who need the assistance. Steinberg is known for only taking on clients who agree to donate a portion of their salaries to charity. And with the salaries of today's top sports stars climbing through the ozone layer, those portions add up to a whole pile of money going to worthy charities. As Steinberg says, humbly, "We're all responsible in some way for the shape the world is in."

I have never doubted that we were put on this earth to help one another, to hold each other up. Turn to the acknowledgments page in this book and look at the list of people I formally recognize, and give thanks to, for their support and encouragement. All have touched me in a special way at one point or another throughout my life and my career. What we do for ourselves—and each other—while we are here will either fade into obscurity or, ideally, be recognized as some kind of contribution. You can either let life pass you by and go unnoticed or try to make a difference, to give back to others.

As successful businesspeople and entrepreneurs, we have plenty of opportunities to give back and help someone else. Michael Vann, an owner of the Shark Bar, a popular New York restaurant (and celebrity hangout), tries to offer troubled youths a different path by preaching the promise of entrepreneurship. He has hired a couple of young adults with criminal pasts and has trained them in the business of running a restaurant. Vann hopes that his protégés will someday go into business for themselves.

Eddie Murphy has also donated countless dollars and much time to a number of worthwhile charities. Yet he, too, prefers to do this quietly, and I will not go against his wishes by expounding on this further. I will, however, tell you one story of how he was able to brighten the life of one young person. And I have to admit that this also affected me deeply.

As you can imagine, Eddie receives thousands of requests from organizations and individuals seeking some sort of assistance—financial and otherwise. Of course, he can't respond positively to every situation—it's just not possible. But once in a while there comes a very special—and heart-wrenching—request that seems impossible to turn down. One such plea came to us through the James Lyons Foundation. A fourteen-year-old boy was dying of leukemia, and he had said that his last wish was to meet Eddie. Unfortunately Eddie was in the middle of a project and couldn't get away. So what we did do was have Eddie record a message on a cassette and sign a poster and photograph for the boy. I took the package to Memorial Sloan-Kettering and spent time with the boy and his aunt. I must say it was a bit difficult for me to go back to that hospital—I had counseled quite a few patients there during my days as a social worker, and it brought back a lot of disheartening memories. The next day the mother called to tell me how much the gifts meant to the young man—he had slept with the tape recorder under his pillow and asked his mother to take care of the gifts Eddie had given him. He knew he was dying. I was genuinely touched and glad that we could do something that made the boy's last days a little brighter. When he did pass away, the mother said later, he was smiling as he looked at Eddie's photograph.

In all the years I've represented Eddie, I think this was one of the most important things I've done. That's what life on the planet is all about, folks: being there for one another whenever, or however, we can. Box office numbers, the gold records, all pale in comparison with being able to send someone "home" with a smile on their face.

My buddy Richard Lawson, the former *All My Children* actor whom I "rescued" before a basketball game, has seen his share of challenges and hardships, not to mention "near death" experiences. He's survived a couple of terrible auto accidents, *and* he was one of the passengers on that ill-fated USAir flight a few years ago in New York, the one that skidded off the runway during takeoff and crashed, killing about twenty people. Richard was one of the lucky ones, and even though he's been through enough hard times himself, he knows the joys of "giving back." He is constantly donating his time to a number of charitable organizations, and he travels the country (overcoming his fear of flying) as part of his duties as spokesman for the NBA Players Association antidrug program.

As I mentioned before, the inner joy one gets from giving back or helping out should be a reward in itself. In other words, do something nice simply because it's a nice thing to do, not because you may gain some type of celebrity from your actions. Menshach Taylor, the actor who was on television's *Designing Women* and is now on *Dave's World,* has often said that people sometimes react negatively to his benevolence and outwardly altruistic behavior. They think he's putting on some kind of "holier than thou" act. But he genuinely loves the feeling of helping people, so he just keeps on keepin' on.

It's a great feeling to make someone feel better or smile. (It's the social worker in me peeking through here.) Try it. You'll find out. The late Bill Bixby, who starred in a number of hit television series over the last three decades, discovered the joy of giving of himself even when he was battling cancer. In an article in *TV Guide,* Bixby said: "You know, the most meaningful part of being in the hospital was meeting the other patients. A nurse asked me to visit another patient—it was a woman who'd been fighting cancer for God knows how long. She'd been through chemotheraphy and had just lost her leg to surgery. So I grabbed the flowers Bob Newhart sent to me and went to see her. And when she saw my face she went, 'Oh!' and smiles this incredible smile, she was so happy to see me. And I just sat on the bed and held her and rocked her. At that moment, she forgot she had lost her leg. That's when I knew that what we do is important."

Volunteer your time and services, but do so selectively. I've often had to resign from the boards of various institutions and organizations because I found that I was overextending myself. A precaution: Don't be hasty to join up or sign on if indeed you can't—in good conscience—fulfill your commitments. Shallow offerings are just that . . . shallow. And remember that your actions speak much louder than your words.

But don't be discouraged. There are a zillion organizations out there that would benefit from a helping hand—either in terms of a charitable donation or of time spent working as a volunteer. In fact, volunteerism is a way of life for many businesspeople today, despite their frenzied schedules at work and at home. Many folks are finding that their lives are lacking somehow and discover that helping to make someone else's life better fills that gap. How? The ideas and opportunities are endless. Here are a few examples to get you thinking:

- Help out with a children's program at the local Y or at your church. Remember our future—helping out with kids will guarantee us all a better tomorrow.
- Head down to a soup kitchen or shelter that provides food for the homeless and help to prepare the meals. Anyone can chop vegetables, boil some potatoes. At holiday time go a step further and "adopt" a needy family. It won't cost much to provide a Thanksgiving or Christmas turkey and a couple of small gifts for the

children. And you can turn what would have been a dismal holiday into a joyful experience for some people who are less fortunate.

• Don't just throw out those old clothes—or the ones that don't fit anymore. Take a moment to pack them up and bring them down to a shelter or even distribute them yourself to those who must live on the street.

• Use your managerial or office skills to organize a group that will work together for a particular charity. Enlist your co-workers and plan a once-a-month (or more frequent) visit to a shelter or youth home.

And I don't want to hear that you are "too busy" to get involved with something that would help make a difference for other people. *The New York Times* once devoted a whole column on the "executive life" that told of top business executives—incredibly busy people!—who have gotten involved with coaching youngsters in Little League baseball. As one manager said, "Even though it sounds corny, I get tremendous gratification out of doing something I know contributes to the fabric of my neighborhood."

Chapter 28

Cultivating Our Future

When we first opened the doors to the Agency—and remember that we were doing this on a shoestring—I quickly learned the value of employing part-time workers and interns. One thing I could count on was what seemed like a never-ending supply of young people eager to lend a hand, volunteer their services, and generally help out around the office, all in exchange for a stipend and the chance to make important connections and to learn about the business. And I must admit that we were never afraid to put them right to work—and I mean *work*. Slave labor? Well, not really, although I'm sure some of those who have passed through our offices may have felt that way. I am of the opinion that if you tell me that you want to do entertainment PR, then I assume you mean just that and *all* that goes into becoming the best. So you will work, and learn, because I will not accept anything less than your best. But the key point here is that I give as good as I get. Sure, their work for me helps *me* out. But, more important, it helps them. It helps them focus their aspirations, it gives them concrete experience, it gives them ideas for their futures. The world—our world—is on their shoulders. So teach them well!

I have always found that I have a special fondness for young people—I simply like dealing with them. Their enthusiasm, eagerness, and willingness to learn is a constant source of inspiration. And today I know there is a whole generation of PR wannabes—young entrepreneurs—out there who are creating their own opportunities and seeking a more productive and successful life. If I have had the opportunity to touch these young people in some way, I feel blessed for having been able to do so.

At any given time at the Agency, we may have as many as six young people working as interns. Most are students, but we've also had the pleasure of working with some young professionals—even lawyers and writers—who are looking to change careers. Some have even taken major cuts in their salaries or have traveled across the country just for an interview. It's a "one hand washes the other" situation, mostly. They are looking for experience, and we can always use an extra pair of hands.

But how do we find all these eager, willing-to-work-for-almost-nothing, talented folks? Basically it happens because I am consistently "out there," meeting and greeting people, speaking at seminars, schools, and business gatherings. And I try to make sure that we stay in touch on some level with those I meet and come in contact with. Say I've just spoken at a gathering—which would be attended by professionals and students alike—and I've given my standard speech on "marketing yourself." The crowd seems to heed my advice because no sooner am I wrapping up my talk than I'm surrounded by what seems like the entire group, asking for more information, offering their cards or their résumés, or simply wanting to chat. If, perhaps, I simply don't have the time to speak with everyone at that particular moment, I encourage them to contact me or my staff via a letter or phone call.

Anyone who does reach out to me gets a response, without fail. I or a staff member will either return the phone call or respond to the letter with a call or a note attached to the latest copy of the Agency newsletter or a kit on the company. And I'll invite them to hang out at the Agency (translation: work) if they want. Or if they can't take the time for that, they're welcome to ride with me in taxis so they can share at least those fifteen minutes of my time. Or we regularly invite people to work/attend an event the Agency is handling, and I'll find the time to chat during a break or after the event is over—and I'll introduce them to the various "family" members of staff, volunteers, and interns so that there is a valuable exchange of information. And I ask for something in return: that they do the same for others as they move on in their business travels. Chris Cathcart, a friend and former Agency executive who now heads up the New York publicity department at Motown Records, and Susan Nowak, whom I mentioned earlier, are exemplary of that. They reach out to people and "pass it on."

We are all painfully aware that we are losing our children to drugs, crime, the streets, apathy. Never was this more horrifyingly evident to me than when I read a quote from a teenager who was involved with the infamous "Hail Mary" murder of another teen. The boy involved said that participating in the murder was the first thing he'd "accomplished" in his young life. "I don't like that a person died while I accomplished something," he said, "but he did."

This is a mind-numbing and tragic message. We as a nation are desperately failing our youth. And we must start looking to the future, or there will be no future. We have to give our youth alternatives. And I challenge everyone who reads this book to truly reflect on what that teenager said. Someone had to die in order for him to feel a sense of accomplishment.

One woman in Detroit took it upon herself to try and make a difference in her hometown. Clementine Barfield, whose one son was killed and another shot in the random violence of the urban streets, organized hundreds of bereaved parents, community leaders, and concerned citizens into the now nationally renowned antiviolence group Save Our Sons and Daughters. The group offers counseling to surviving family members of those caught up in the violence and organizes vigils, marches, rallies, and lobbying for gun control. Save Our Sons and Daughters has become a major force for change in Detroit and a model of community-based organizing for the rest of the country.

> *I am only one, but still I am one. I cannot do everything, but still I can do something. And because I cannot do everything I will not refuse to do the something that I can do.*
>
> —Edward Everett Hale

Newspapers around the country are also doing their part to lend a hand. The *Detroit Free Press* has launched Children First, a project that does everything from chronicling urban tragedy to sending kids to summer camp and even organizing lawyers—at no charge!—to help at-risk kids. And other publications like the *Chicago Tribune, Washington Post,* and *Chicago Sun-Times* are waging crusades against the violence by pledging that no child-related tragedy goes unnoticed and by rallying community leaders.

I challenge you, and ask you to challenge others, to become a mentor to young people. Allow someone to shadow you—follow you around for a day, sit in on meetings, get a feel for who you are and what you do. It costs nothing to develop these relationships, and I guarantee you that you'll reap untold benefits. So will the person to whom you've devoted some time. A recent Lou Harris poll indicated that 73 percent of students said mentors helped them raise their goals and expectations. Eighty-seven percent of high school students who had the chance to be guided by someone went on to college or planned to within a year of graduating. And of all students polled, 59 percent showed improved grades after having had a mentor.

The children are our future. We must all strive to work together and ensure that the road to tomorrow is properly paved for those who will follow us. Mentoring is one way to pass on what we've learned and to give back some of our blessings and advantages.

Be mindful, too, that the style of mentoring is changing today as we see a tougher, more experienced group of young people entering the work force. The traditional view of mentoring is that a senior-level person selects a promising newcomer to the company and then proceeds with a lot of personal, one-on-one, caring advice and leadership that helps the young person along. The mentor is understanding and encouraging—should a protégé make a mistake, the mentor is there to pick him up, brush him off, and offer words of reassurance. And this traditional style still holds true—in most cases, but not all. Many of today's promising newcomers may not need as much hand holding. Their confidence seems higher, and they may bounce back from a mistake much quicker than you'd think, probably because of the higher quality of business education. Most students today feel better prepared because they *are*. Many have worked at various companies while going to school and have had a true look at the "real world." They know what they're up against.

These kids can be tough. You should act accordingly,

mixing encouragement with high demands and stimulating assignments. I think of it as a responsibility and an obligation. And the most powerful possibility for a better future: each one, teach one.

Perhaps you may not have the time to be a full-blown mentor to one person. No problem! I don't believe in working with just one person at a time, anyway. Divide what time you do have among a number of young people. A few minutes here and there *will* be appreciated. And if you're truly committed to giving back, you will find the opportunity somehow.

I was once out of town with a client and had scheduled a hectic, filled-to-the-brim day of meetings. A former intern, Jocelyn Coleman, now a reporter for a local Gannett newspaper, had kept in touch and knew I'd be visiting this certain city, where two of her friends happened to be starting their own public relations business. Would I mind, she asked, meeting with them briefly? Of course not, I said, and we set up a time in the evening to meet at my hotel. Of course, the day's event took much, much longer than I had expected, and I didn't get back to my hotel until almost midnight. The two young entrepreneurs, however, had waited for me. Even though I was dragging, I knew that I could not turn them away. So we went up to my room where we chatted until well after one in the morning. And as tired as I was, I still felt good after our meeting. Passing it on always puts a smile on my face.

Jocelyn, by the way, has done an incredible job of staying in touch and on top of news and information. She gives back to me by being a wealth of timely info, some of which I've been able to use in some of my speeches. It's a two-way street.

Chapter 29

Learning from Others

Learning from others is one of the best tools for success. I want to give you a few special examples of how people can make a difference: some people who have had a lasting impact on my life, my work, and my success and a few people whom I have yet to meet but have admired from afar. Let me point out that we're just scratching the surface here—this is merely a sampling. But I hope that these stories may inspire you in some ways, and challenge you in others. Learn from these examples. Find a way to make your own difference. A wise person once said, "If you think one person cannot bring about meaningful change in this world, think again."

We constantly read, see, and hear about world leaders or policy makers who are trying to make a difference—good or bad; they get the "ink" and the television and radio coverage. But thousands of stories of people who are making their own difference never get into the spotlight; these are the true unsung heroes.

For example, there's the man who got so angry when New York City grocers harassed street people trying to redeem aluminum cans that he used his life savings and devoted all his time to establish a redemption center catering to, and staffed by, the homeless. There is now less litter and trash in his neighborhood, and many redeemers have used the earnings to restart their lives.

There's also Ed Cooper, a Boston man who noticed that many of his neighbors had to skimp on food to pay their heating bills and persuaded city officials to let residents convert city-owned lots into vegetable gardens. The result: Boston Urban Gardens has established almost 150 such gardens.

Cora Lee Johnson of Soperton, Georgia, got angry when she heard local officials wanted to return federal housing funds because they didn't think poor people deserved public housing. She went over their heads, pressing Congress and federal officials on behalf of the town's poor. Her efforts led to the construction of apartments to house thirty impoverished families.

Mike Bernardo, a veteran record industry executive, is also a true humanitarian. She (that's right, her name is Mike. See, I wasn't kidding when I stressed the importance of checking out names before contacting a person!) was the first Black woman to be named a regional promotions marketing manager at CBS Records. During her career, she has worked with such superstars as Miles Davis and Patti LaBelle. She has also raised thirteen children—three she gave birth to and ten adoptees. And she and her husband founded the 331 Foundation, a Washington, D.C.-based organization that provides families with medical assistance, educational development, and cultural and religious development. The "331" comes from the number of women who were slain in D.C. during 1991. After reading a news story that reported this horrific fact, Mike decided she had to do something to make a difference in the lives of the children left behind. Let me be the first to tell you she most definitely has.

Anyone who sees a problem can do something to fix it or bring about a change that will effect a cure. But it takes persistence (and we've already seen what that can do), a plan, and a willingness to stick your neck out. Get over the passivity and apathy and at least try. Choose one problem and act on it. Ask yourself: What single issue or circumstance bothers and/or affects you the most? What do you wish were different? Most likely there are already groups or organizations set up and taking steps to alter a certain situation. If not, launch your own. Remember that even a modest effort can bring about meaningful change.

Before you begin your attack, do your homework. Were there similar problems in the past, maybe faced by another community or group? What was their solution? And how can their efforts be improved upon? Get background information on the company or industry you may be going after—what are they doing, what have they done? Be prepared to offer realistic alternatives backed up with research. Enlist the support of others: begin a letter-writing campaign or make phone calls to those who may be willing to help. (Remember the importance of building and maintaining contacts. A well-connected person will have a much better chance of getting people to respond to a request for assistance. Knowing people is at least as useful in getting help on others' behalf as it is in getting something for yourself.)

Leah Wilcox is a special kind of person. As director of player and talent relations for NBA (National Basketball Association) Entertainment, Leah is in constant touch with all the players in the game. And the players respond to Leah because her personality is a unique blend of street savvy and professionalism. Leah is always there to help, and she will—as much as possible—enlist the services of players to assist in a charitable effort. Often they do it simply because Leah has asked them to. Her work with the popular "NBA Stay in School Jam" has helped bring together the players and has helped kids around the country by teaching them the benefits of an education. Leah exhibits many of the important and righteous qualities mentioned in this book and has honed her skills and abilities to transform herself from a "street-smart girl" to a key asset in the billion-dollar organization that is the NBA—and she is fun.

Reverend Johnny Ray Youngblood is pastor of the St. Paul Community Baptist Church, located in the East New York section of Brooklyn, one of the most desolate urban communities in America. One of the reverend's favorite sweatshirts is emblazoned with the legend "JUST DO IT." This dynamic spiritual leader certainly does. As co-chairman of the East Brooklyn Congregations, Reverend Youngblood helped found the Nehemiah Project (named after the biblical prophet who rebuilt the walls of Jerusalem), which built 2,300 affordable homes for low-income familes; he formed an alliance with city banks to secure jobs for Black high school graduates—hundreds have gained entry-level positions; he has engaged in an aggressive campaign to bring men into his church, delivering the message "Ladies, we love you. Children, we are proud of you. But, men, we need you."

The Black church is often the pillar of the African-American community, and Youngblood is at the forefront in expanding the church's role to assume responsibilities abdicated by many of our country's failing institutions. Youngblood's work has been chronicled in a book entitled *Upon This Rock: The Miracles of a Black Church* (the Agency provided publicity services for the release of the book, published by HarperCollins), which documents the incredible challenges that are part of the everyday experience for those who live in the beleaguered community that is East New York. Reverend Youngblood uses inspiration, determination, and guidance as his weapons to combat these daily battles. He sticks his neck out every day, challenging the city's bureaucratic policies, the people of his neighborhood, other high-profile ministers, and even the traditions of religion itself.

Yet as writer Lawrence H. Mamiya said, "Men like Reverend Youngblood *stand out* as beacons of hope and anchors of their community. *Human, all too human,* but also miraculous." Check out the phrases I put in italics. Notice the correlation with the themes I've been presenting over the last few chapters?

Zeke Mowatt, the former professional football player, is one of the finest human beings I've ever met. He has a heart of gold. Yet, you may remember, Zeke was at the center of a tremendous controversy a few years back when he and other members of his NFL team were alleged to have harassed a female reporter who was in the players' locker room. Throughout the whole ordeal, Zeke never talked to the press (on the advice of his attorneys) and was consistently maligned. He suffered the loss of his reputation, a fortune in legal fees, and most likely any chance of redeeming himself in the remaining years of his career.

When Zeke was playing ball, he didn't really come across as the typical nice guy athlete. He rarely spoke to the press, was quiet and kind of kept to himself, and on the field was a very rough player. Therefore he was perceived as standoffish and maybe even nasty by the fans, the press, and sometimes even his teammates.

Truth is—and I've known the guy for almost seven years—he doesn't smoke, drink, or do drugs. He doesn't even curse. In fact, if he's telling a story and has to repeat some profanity that someone else used, he spells it out!

I'm serious—you see this big, fine hunk of a man saying something like "Well, this one guy said he didn't give a s-h-i-t." This is not a guy who would have said those things—or performed those actions—that allegedly took place in that locker room. To give you a couple of examples of what he's truly like: Once there was a young boy in Zeke's church (Zeke attends church every Sunday without fail) who had tried to commit suicide. The pastor asked Zeke to spend some time with the boy. Zeke had the boy and his sister over to his house, helping them with their homework. The two were living with their grandparents, who couldn't afford to give the kids nice clothes or presents. And although Zeke certainly could do that, he refrained because he knew that it wouldn't be right—it might displace the grandparents. However, when the occasion arose he was quick to spread his generosity to disadvantaged kids. One Christmas Day he was scheduled to have ten kids from the local orphanage spend a day at his house. At midnight he got a call from the orphanage, asking if he could take one more kid who was left behind by relatives. Again he didn't hesitate to say yes. He even went out and got a gift for the kid, to add to the ones for the other children who would be there. Once when he and I went to the movies in the dead of winter—below zero, ice everywhere—we saw a young man with cerebral palsy trying to walk with his braces over the ice. We never even discussed it; Zeke instinctively reached out to the guy, and we ended up walking him four blocks out of our way. Zeke even carried him several feet since the braces kept slipping on the ice.

Here's a man who is constantly making a difference in people's lives. And he does all that not in spite of the personal challenges he faced, but simply because that's the kind of human being he is.

We can all be better people if we emulate the good deeds

of others. Conversely, another way to succeed is to take inspiration from those who *don't* impress you. Sounds weird, right? But listen—anyone can be impressed or inspired by the successful person who has righteously earned a place at the top. However, take a look at someone who has perhaps "made it" for some or all of the wrong reasons. Be fueled by that: tell yourself, "If they can do it, be it, have it . . . I certainly can." Remember that former actor who used to be in the White House? The man was known to nod off during meetings, for God's sake. Talk about being a little out of touch! And he held the most important position of power on the planet. I constantly drew inspiration from him, saying to myself, "If he can be in that position and do that . . there's *no way* I can't try to run this little business of mine." He was a constant reminder that I could do whatever I set my mind to.

You can, too.

We can all be there for each other and, by even the smallest of courtesies, help someone along the way. But it's important to note that if you're lending a hand or devoting yourself to a cause *simply* and *solely* for the resulting celebrity that may result by your actions . . . well, as they say in New York, fuhgeddaboudit. You're in the wrong business.

As an example, let me share with you a tale of people making a difference. Courtland Milloy, a columnist for *The Washington Post,* once wrote a story about a homeless family: an elderly father and his three young children who were living in an abandoned building. After the story was published, Milloy was flooded with phone calls and letters from people who wanted to send donations and offers of help. Within a couple of weeks, the family had moved out of their squalor into the home of a woman who simply said, "I'm old-fashioned. I'm a great believer that unless individuals do something to help, nothing is going to change. I don't have a lot of money. But I have been blessed with a home, so I decided to share that." The family had also received an offer to move into their own three-bedroom apartment; the real estate agent who made the gesture asked to remain anonymous, as did many of those who contributed thousands of dollars to the family.

Jim Brown, the legendary football player, left the game while he was still at the top of his form. Arguably the greatest running back in football history, he could have extended his career to earn more money and get all he could for himself. Instead, in the years since he left the game, he has worked tirelessly to make a difference. Today, the activist and humanitarian is the nerve center for a rehabilitation program called AMER-I-CAN, which works with former gang members and young men who have been incarcerated. The management of life skills classes of the program are held in facilities in seven states, trains over thirteen thousand men, and is available to inmates preparing to reenter society, gang members who might otherwise be destined for prison, and kids from the ghetto.

Brown became the prototype football player through a combination of determination, strength, and willpower, and he has called upon all these qualities to lend credibility to the program that is pioneering across this country in a most positive, "make a difference" style.

Here are a few more examples of folks who try to make a difference because they want to, not because of the hype they may get:

John Lucas, the former NBA player and former coach of the San Antonio Spurs, was destined for basketball superstardom. He was an athletic prodigy as a child, excelling in two sports: he played tennis at Wimbledon at fifteen, and he was an All-American in basketball at the University of Maryland. In 1976, he became an instant millionaire when he was the first player selected by the Houston Rockets in the NBA draft. Soon after, however, Lucas fell into a tailspin of alcohol, drug abuse, and serious trouble.

Over the next ten years he would play for half a dozen teams and never truly live up to his awesome talent. In 1986, after hitting rock bottom, he began a new life of sobriety and realized that his experiences could possibly help others. Over the next four years, until he retired from playing in 1990, Lucas built a network that would become the prototype of the NBA's substance abuse program. Since 1986 he has operated the Houston, Texas–based John H. Lucas Enterprises, a substance abuse recovery program for athletes. He is also the owner of the U.S. Basketball League's Miami Tropics, a team designed to give recovering addicts a chance to resume their athletic careers.

John Lucas has proven himself a winner on the basketball court and off. He has made a difference by saving lives. As he once said, "I believe in miracles because I am one."

Another former basketball player, Bob Love, is also a true inspiration. Today, any stranger listening to Love talk about his job as a member of the NBA's Chicago Bulls' front office would find him warm, articulate, and friendly. Anyone who has known him for many years, however, would find his conversation astonishing. You see, Love also sank into poverty and despair after 1977, when he retired from the NBA. But in this case it wasn't drugs. The fact was that since the time Love was a child—coming from a broken, abusive homelife—he had suffered from a severe stuttering problem. And when his playing days were over, his speech impediment kept him from getting a good job, even though he had always done well in school and had a degree.

After years of frustration, Love finally found a speech therapist who helped him with his problem. And, using his favorite phrase, "You gotta believe," Love struggled to overcome his affliction. At the age of forty-five he made his first speech at a sports banquet, and for thirty minutes he talked—without stuttering—of realizing dreams and never giving up.

The crowd gave him a standing ovation—twice. Now he gives over two hundred speeches a year and spends a lot of his time answering mail from other stutterers who consider him an inspiration.

George Raveling, the coach of the USC basketball team, regularly sends batches of newspaper and periodical clippings to his players, staff, friends, and colleagues. I met him once five years ago, and I continue to be on his list.

On his own time, Raveling compiles his "Reading for Black Folks," which includes articles about issues of interest for the curious and informed reader. A small gesture from a busy man because he believes it is necessary and helpful. And that's why Raveling is one of the most successful coaches in the country.

You don't have to be a star athlete, or a successful agent, or a television personality, to make a difference. Anyone can effect change and help others—and at any age. Do it in your home, in your neighborhood, in your office. And you can start anytime—you're never too old, never too young. I saw a picture in the newspaper the other day of an eighty-nine-year-old woman being led away by police in handcuffs. Her crime? She was among a group of protesters rallying against the proposed building of a nuclear facility. Getting arrested is a bit extreme, yes. And at eighty-nine? Go get 'em, Grandma! You can bet she's getting her point across!

Then there's Nathan Talbot, an eighteen-year-old from Syracuse, New York, I read about a while back. At sixteen Nathan joined an organization called HIPP, an acronym for Help Increase the Peace Program. He got so interested in the program that he signed up for advanced workshops and training so he could help lead the seminars, which he has done for over a year. Here's a kid who is certainly making a difference, giving up his precious weekends and other spare time to help other people.

All of us, young and old, celebrity and not-so-famous—we are all human, and we're on the planet for each other.

Afterword

Few burdens are heavy when everybody lifts.

—AFRICAN PROVERB

What's the magic that causes certain men and women to succeed where those of equal intelligence fail? To have an edge, stand out, and never forget the personal touch!

That's what it's all about. Sometimes this stuff sounds corny. So? Wherever you are in life, you can give something to someone. Remember to be a good person. You *can* make a difference. And believe me, you *can* change your life. Look at what an "average" girl like me has been able to do.

Once, after I gave a speech in Louisville, Kentucky, a young woman came up to me and said that she really hoped one day people would want to listen to what she had to say. I laughed, because my thought was, Who in the world would have thought anyone would come listen to anything *I* have to say? I'm just Terrie, a girl from Mount Vernon.

But now I'm being honored with "keys to the city," and I've been proud to speak for two different organizations at which I was the first woman to do so in seventy-nine and fifty-five years, respectively. You never know!

So, surely, I told the woman, they will want to listen to you one day. Just watch! Count on it.

You, too, can do it. It's in your hands. I challenge you. Stay strong.

20 Ways to Promote Yourself in Business*

Imagine this: A producer from *Oprah* is looking for secretaries to talk about their jobs on an upcoming program. A writer from your local newspaper is doing a story on single mothers who successfully manage a full-time job and a family. Would *you* get the call to appear on the show or to be interviewed for the article? Consider that for every worthwhile business endeavor, there are at least ten other qualified people with the same set of credentials. How will you distinguish yourself? What will you say, what will you do, that will ensure that *you* stand out, are recognized, and ultimately take the top prize? What seeds have you planted for success?

The ability and willingness to master a combination of the "little things" can set you apart from others. Most people greatly underestimate the importance of business details and do not take the time to establish the proper

*This is a slightly different version of an article that was published in 1988.

mind-set they need to employ them. But whether you are a job beginner or an established executive, you can stand out among the crowd if you totally embrace and practice these twenty "little things."

1. **Know that your reputation is valuable**—and that it often reaches people before you do. With that in mind, understand the importance of how you interact with people. Be sincere, be honest, be prepared, be professional, be thorough, be efficient—and deliver.
2. **Do what you say you're going to do.** Getting noticed takes hard work—but it's a very small part of the total picture. If you can't deliver on time (and reasons for this should have to do only with circumstances beyond your control), then pick up the phone ASAP and say so. And make sure you meet the next deadline you've set.
3. **Return *all* phone calls** or make sure someone in your organization returns them. You never know why a person may be calling.
4. **Treat everyone with respect and courtesy.** A person's position in life should have absolutely nothing to do with how you interact with them. What goes around, comes around.
5. **Be visible.** Go to professional seminars, luncheons, receptions, dinners, any kind of gathering of folks. Don't be afraid to attend a function alone—you may find you know someone when you get there. And if you don't, you'll meet someone. The point is, you have to be out there for people to notice you.
6. **When you meet people, be mindful.** Look them in the eye, smile, be personable, have a firm handshake (few things are worse than one of those limp, dishrag handshakes—you know the kind!), and ac-

tually *be* with the individual at that moment. And just a little aside: Research studies show that people who smile are perceived as more intelligent than people who don't.

7. **Try to develop a knack for remembering names.** People you meet will be flattered if you can call them by name after only a brief introduction. You *can* master the knack for easy memorization. It's all based on the fact that your recall is best when you want to remember, when the words are simple, and when you reinforce them with repetition. Here's how:

   • Set your priorities before you meet with a new group of people. Figure out whom you want to meet and why. This will motivate you.

   • If you need to know first names and not last names, or vice versa, concentrate on the part you need.

   • As you meet each new person, say his or her name aloud. Repeat the name in your head several times as you look at the person.
8. **Be an active listener** while you're engaging in conversation. If you feel yourself becoming bored or distracted, just politely excuse yourself.
9. **Create a "small talk" notebook** for when you go out. This will contain anecdotes and/or questions you jot down about life or current events that are guaranteed to stimulate conversation. Be creative—even outrageous—but always professional with your ideas. Take a look at your notes before you go to a function, and be ready. Another surefire conversation starter: Ask people something about themselves. People do like to talk about their own lives and jobs and to share their experiences.
10. **Be sensitive to the body language** of those you

come in contact with. And be careful of how you come across to other people. Maybe it's not the right time to strike up a conversation. On the other hand, perhaps you'll notice a person at a gathering who seems to be alone. You might bring her into the center of things. If you are the leader of an organization, you'll have an eager, committed worker for life! People remember special treatment.

11. **Send a follow-up note** to people you meet and would like to stay in touch with—say hello, enjoyed meeting with you, mention a mutual area of interest or something noteworthy about the encounter and the possibility of getting together in the future.
12. **Get to know the support staff** of the person or company you might want to do business with. It costs you nothing to develop these relationships, and when you call, there'll be a better chance of being put through.
13. **Know your profession.** Stay abreast of all the latest trends and developments in your field and your geographic area. Read everything you can get your hands on and know who is doing what, where, when, and how. Include daily newspapers in your area and from selected areas across the country (there are newsstands that specialize in foreign and out-of-state publications) and general-interest and specialized magazines. Learn the art of skimming—you won't be able to read everything thoroughly.
14. **Pass articles along with a note** if you come across one that may be of interest to a co-worker or colleague. I had small cards printed with the message "I thought you might find the enclosed of interest," with my name, company, address, and phone number. Maybe your associates don't have or don't take the time to read the number of publications you

do. Be their eyes. You'll provide a valuable and unforgettable service that they will undoubtedly appreciate.

15. **Keep a supply of greeting cards for all occasions**—marriage, birthday, new baby, death, anniversary (job, marriage), thanks, sorry, blank (just to say hello). Pay attention to the special occasions (honors, appointments, promotions) of colleagues and prospective business contacts—and stay in touch.
16. **Write . . . write . . . write.** Send letters to people you want to do business with. Say "hello," "congratulations," "I like your work/your style/your recent remarks/your article." Many valuable professional relationships I've developed came about this way. For example, I once sent a simple letter to the owner of one of the hottest private clubs in New York after I'd seen him host an awards program, and it resulted in complimentary membership for me in both his New York and London clubs.
17. **Go through your Rolodex periodically** and send a hello note to those people who you want to remember you. Maybe it's been a while since you chatted. Keep your name and that of your company in front of them.
18. **Let people know that you are available to speak** or to otherwise participate in panel discussions, seminars, clubs, religious organizations, civic groups, charitable organizations, service groups, and community centers.
19. **Selectively donate your services** to nonprofit organizations that may be in need of your expertise. Set the stage for people to get to know who you are and what you do.
20. **Remember what Mom used to tell you—say**

"thank you." It's amazing how few people invest the time to express gratitude for a favor or a job well done. Remember that people don't have to do anything for you.

It's all about developing a winning style and cultivating relationships that can be instrumental in opening doors you never dreamed could open for you. Work hard to achieve your goals. Understand that there will be disappointments and defeats along with the highs and the joyous victories, but if you apply the "little things," you'll be amazed at how many "big things" may result!

Suggested Reading

BOOKS

The Celestine Prophecy, An Adventure, James Redfield, Warner Books.

Female Fortunes: Lessons from the 100 Greatest Women Entrepreneurs of Our Day, A. David Silver, AMACOM.

Diamond in the Rough, Barry J. Farber, the Putnam/Berkley Publishing Group.

Getting Back to the Basics of Public Relations and Publicity, Matthew J. Culligan and Dolph Greene.

Growing a Business, Paul Hawken, Simon & Schuster.

Making Connections, Carol Gilligan, Nona Lyons, Trudy Hanner, eds., Harvard University Press.

Marketing Yourself, Dorothy Leeds, HarperCollins.

On Becoming a Leader, Warren Bennis, Addison-Wesley Publishers (Reading, Mass.).

Rogers' Rules for Success, Henry C. Rogers, St. Martin's Press.

Scrambling—Zig-Zagging Your Way to the Top, Elwood N. Chapman, J. P. Tarcher, Inc./Houghton Mifflin Company.

Success Runs in Our Race: The Complete Guide to Effective Networking in the African American Community, George C. Fraser, William Morrow Company.

The Practice of Public Relations, Fraser Seitel, Macmillan Publishing.

Think and Grow Rich, Dennis Kimbro and Napoleon Hill, Fawcett Crest Publishing.

PERIODICALS

Jack O'Dwyer's Newsletter: 271 Madison Ave., New York, N.Y. 10016.

Public Relations Career Directory, Career Press Inc.: P.O. Box 34, Hawthorne, N.J. 07507.

Public Relations News, Phillips Business Information, Inc.: 305 Madison Ave., Suite 4417, New York, N.Y. 10165.

Successfully Launching a Public Relations Firm, Information Center (Public Relations Society of America): 33 Irving Place, New York, N.Y. 10003.

Appendix: Unique Books, Cards, Art, and So Forth— And Where to Find Them

BOOKS

Acts of Faith, Iyanla Vanzant, Fireside Books (a division of Simon & Schuster).

Black Pearls (daily meditations, affirmations and inspirations for African Americans), Eric Copage, William Morrow & Company.

Book of Questions; *Make Beliefs: A Gift for Your Imagination*; *Lifelines: A Book of Hope*, William Zimmerman, Guarionex Press, (212) 724-5259.

Daily Word (book of daily meditations and inspirations), Daily Word, Unity Village, Mo. 64065, 1-800-669-0282.

The Giving Tree, Shel Silverstein, Harper & Row.

Life's Little Instruction Book, H. Jackson Brown, Jr., Rutledge Hill Press, Nashville, Tenn.

Secrets of Life, J. Donald Walters, Warner Books.

Tapping the Power Within, Iyanla Vanzant, Harlem River Press.

Bob Law's Children's Book Store, 225 DeKalb Ave., Brooklyn, N.Y. 11217, 1-718-596-6603.

UNIQUE CARDS

Pat Kabore: 17334 Meyers, Detroit, Mich. 48235, 1-313-342-1683.

Studio 29, Ruth Springer: 15516 Sunset Blvd., Pacific Palisades, Calif. 90272, 1-310-459-0375.

Posh Papers by Judi Boren: 532 Elmgrove Ave., Providence, R.I. 02906.

Nancy Brandon: 65 W. 90th St., New York, N.Y. 10024, 1-212-580-8578.

Frederick Douglass Designs: 1033 Folger Ave., Berkeley, Calif. 94710, 1-510-204-0950.

EthnoGraphics: 3463 State St., Suite 142, Santa Barbara, Calif. 93105, 1-805-687-9483.

Souls Food: P.O. Box 90522, Atlanta, Ga. 30364, 1-404-209-8088.

UNIQUE ART

L. B. Davis Gallery: 185 Van Rensselaer Blvd., Bldg. 2, #2B, Menands, N.Y. 12204, 1-518-436-9536.

UNIQUE GIFTS

Pannier: 410 Central Park West, 11th floor, New York, N.Y. 10025, 1-212-678-2770.

Laurel Burch Galleries: P.O. Box 2587, Carmel, Calif. 92921, 1-408-626-2822.

Daphne's: 473 Amsterdam Ave., New York, N.Y. 10024.

UNIQUE NOVELTY ITEMS

Gaddy Gear: 478 San Vicente Blvd., Los Angeles, Calif. 90048, 1-213-658-5999.

Pat Kabore: See under Unique Cards.

UNIQUE FLOWERS

Daily Blossom: 787 Seventh Ave., New York, N.Y. 10019, 1-212-554-4600.

Acknowledgments

I'm a human being, just as you are—a living, breathing member of the human race. I also happen to be a person who has been enormously blessed, and I have been able to reach a level of success beyond my wildest expectations.

I did none of this alone.

I am who I am today because of the extraordinary outpouring of love, support, and understanding I've received from many others. They have helped lay the foundation of my being and have helped guide me toward success beyond my imagination.

I'm human. Therefore I have made mistakes. Most of my errors may have been the result of misguided passion or enthusiasm. But I have always tried—with all my heart and with what I had—to do the right thing. And when I have fallen, or felt like giving up, someone has always been there to pick me up, dust off the frustration of failure, and offer words of encouragement and inspiration.

Successes have also been plentiful—made even happier because I can share them with so many.

To the following people . . . I always have appreciated, and always will remember all that you have done for me. The best way I know to say thank you for all you have given me is to pass it on. It is in your names and your spirit that I will forever strive to "give something back" and pass it on to those who will follow us. Do know that you have touched my soul in a way that will be treasured till the end.

With respect and in honor of the ancestors—who sacrificed so much and on whose shoulders I stand . . . Let us continue to work together to win the human race.

To the Creator, from whom all blessings flow.

To my parents: Marie and Charles . . . thank you for giving me the best that you got. All of my love forever.

Mom: A special thanks for telling me I could fly and for holding the net.

Dad: Thank you for opening up and bringing some understanding to this work.

My grandmothers—Laura Basket Kearney Davis and Carrie Bell Williams: I pray that I will have shoulders as broad and be all that you would have been had you lived in a different age and time.

My cousins: Gene Caddy—for the haven (and the shower) and the love; Alexander Williams—for the sweet and gentle spirit and the lifeline; Pat Perry—for planting the very first thought that there was a book in me; Cassandra Alston, Earlene Williams, Wendy Walker, and Shakuwra Muhammad.

Aunt Josephine (Floyd)—for the lifeline.

Susan Taylor—for the ear, the always comforting words, the haven. And for giving the initial inspiration for this book—the "20 points" was your idea, after all.

Helen Goss—for the friendship and wisdom and for lighting the fire to get me started on this book . . . my unofficial coauthor/editor. Here's to peace—and space. Love to Adia.

Joe Cooney—my coauthor—a master wordsmith who made sense of all this and who has been through it all with me . . . your quiet professionalism has always been a rock of support.

Tony Wafford—for the unfailing truth, for making me laugh, for your sense of daring, and for *always* showing me the other side.

And to my sister Lani—for paving the way to my understanding who I am.

Doug Brown—for the uncanny ability to understand.

Chester Burger—for your friendship and guidance and for being one of the first to recognize my talent and that of untold numbers of people of color in the public relations field.

Ken Carter—for the wisdom.

Chris Cathcart—for being my friend and having honor and integrity.

Bill Cosby—for adding that special touch and for caring.

Kenneth Frith—for planting the seeds.

Alan L. Gansberg—for always having the answers and for taking the time.

Ray Gerald—for being the beacon of light that guided me solidly into the future.

Steve Harris—for being my news and information lifeline.

Ramon Hervey—for the guidance and encouragement to make the move.

Cynthia Island, Muntu Law, Kamili Mtume, Vera Pressley, Lauren Slaughter, and Joe Simmons—for sharing your mate with me and the Agency. Words cannot express my gratitude.

Carol Jones—for showing me the ropes and being an anchor.

Jim Kelly—for being the best damn "vice chairman" there ever was.

Bob Law—for trying to keep me on the straight and narrow health road.

Ed Lewis—for waiting, and for always being there.

Victoria Lucas—for being a trailblazer in the industry and passing it on to me.

Jim Moore—for the guidance—and for believing in me.

Zeke Mowatt—for the prayer and generosity of spirit.

Mtume—for your brilliance and the encouragement, and the encouragement, and the encouragement. Put that where you want it.

Eddie Murphy—for your confidence in me and helping me to soar.

Enid Nemy—for helping me to understand that it's the quality of work that counts.

Anna Perez—for being a shining example of excellence, and for the extraordinary unwavering support.

Lester Conner—for the love, inspiration and support.

Henry Rogers—for the book that inspired me and let me know I was indeed on the right track.

Richard Rubinstein *and* his Laurel Entertainment—who judged the Agency on its merits, the first to be oblivious to color.

Carol Salter—for being there all the time—tirelessly.

Vernon Slaughter—for the love, friendship and guidance.

Ken Smikle—all this is the result of your early nagging.

Ken Shropshire—for your love and friendship.

Jae Je Simmons—for your loyalty and vision and for being my sounding board.

Maynell Thomas—for going the extra mile for us.

Jonathan M. Tisch—for your example and your business "seal of approval."

Diana Valdes, Charlotte Floyd Pruitt, Jay Hoggard, Rene McLean—for teaching me the ways of friendship.

Chris Vaughn—for the first Montblanc and the guidance.

To the Warner Books family: Laurence Kirshbaum, Chris Barba, Jamie Brickhouse, Joann Davis, Mauro DiPreta, Maureen Mahon Egen, Diane Ekeblad, Justine Elias, Laura Friedman, Anne Hamilton, Ellen Herrick,

Vincent La Scala, Peter Mauceri, Jacki Merri Meyer, Anne Milburn, Susan Walker Moffat, Cassandra Murray, Tori Nelson, Bruce Paonessa, Mel Parker, Maryann Petyak, Karen Torres, Alexandra Urdang, Nancy Weise—for making my dream become a reality.

To my literary agent, Jeff Herman, who took special effort to get this book published.

To Colleen Kapklein—my editor, who saw and shared the vision and made this maiden voyage into the world of publishing so much easier.

For the guidance:

Clarence Avant, Jack Bernstein, Jim Bowling, Rev. Calvin Butts, Anita Celious, Mayor David N. Dinkins, George Edwards, Les Edwards, Alex English, Toni Fay, Adriane Gaines, Joline Godfrey, Louis Gossett Jr., David and Suzanne Gurwitz, Susan Gwertzman, Rena Hamelfarb, Dr. Allen Hauptman, Rick Jones, Esq., Bernard and Collette King, Richard Lawson, Karen Lee, Dorothy Leeds, Jeanette Lerman, Don Levin, Carolyn Wright Lewis, Leslie Lillien, Lillian and Vernon Lynch, Henry McGee, Dr. Debbie Miller, Sharon Nelson, Ponchitta Pierce, Mildred and Sonny Ray, Dr. Barbara Ross, Robert Shook, Daisy Simmons, William Simmons, Linda Stasi, David Stern, Robin Bell-Stevens, Lemuel Wells, and Nancy Wilson.

For the kind words, support, and inspiration:

Roz Abrams, Colleen Adams, Dottie Anderson, Danny Aiello, Joshua Armstrong, Jeanne Ashe, Carmen Ashhurst, Marilyn Atlas, Rabbi Al Axelrad, Aunt Celeste

(Rainey), Aunt Helen (Williams), Velma Banks, Ornetta Barber, Judy Barker, Carol Bassett, Audrey Bernard, Mike Bernardo, Erieka Bennett, Ted Bennett, Michael Bivins, Tony Blades, Ray Blanco, Kenny, Lola and Bob Blank, Marilyn Bockman, Emma Bowen, Anita and Walter Bridgforth, Avery Brooks, Stanley Brossette, Marie Brown, Richard Brown, Shelley Brown, Tom Brown, Totlee Brown, Vernon Brown, Marjorie Buckner, Raina and Bob Bundy, Khephra Burns, Judie Burstein, Al and JoAnne Caira, Colin Callender, Lee Canaan, Reuben Cannon, Elaine Carter, Shellie Carter, Tony Carter, Linda Casale, Connie Chung, Kelley Chunn, Luther Clark, Chrisena Coleman, Fetteroff Colen, Aldore Collier, Lester Conner, Don Cornelius, Monica Council, Denise Crawford, Evelyn Cunningham, Chris Curry, Lem Daniels, Daphne, Camille and Doc Dattero, Beth Davey, Allison Davis, Suzanne de Passe, Anita DeFrantz, Rev. Richard Dixon, Leslie Doggett, Ofield Duke, Stephanie LaMarre Dyer, Julie Economou, Willie Egyir, Alison Emilio, Steve Epstein, Peggy Esthers, Courtnei Evans, Evelyn Evans, John Feigenbaum, Jose Ferrer, Audrey Fontaine, Cliff Foster, Jeff Fox, Fritz Friedman, Michael Fuchs, Sam and Cynthia Fulwood, Sid Ganis, Brad Gardiner, Gerry and Leslie Geist, Nelson George, Paul Anthony George, Mrs. George, Marla Gibbs, Kay Giorgio, Louis Goldmintz, Christine Gomes, Leslie Gottlieb, Rick Gould, Anthony Gray, Aunt Louise (Green), Phyllis and Ernest Green, Walter Green, Denise Greenawalt, Chris Griffith, Denny Griswold, Aunt Bea (Guy), Leigh Haber, Arsenio Hall, Margaret Hall, Carol Hamilton, Ange-Marie Hancock, Vaughn Harper, Heavy D, Renee Henson, Sue Herzog, Jimmy Hester, Bill Heyman, Yakim and Miriam Himasi, Teresa Holmes, Warrington Hudlin, Karen Hunter Hodge, Rupert Ifil, Bridget Isaac, Iyanla, Lori Jones, Janet Jackson, Ann Jillian, Brad Johnson, Cheese Johnson, Doris

Johnson, Rick Johnson, Roy Johnson, Bill Jones, Loretha Jones, Quincy Jones, Star Jones, Alice Jordan, Pat Kabore, Alan Kannof, Debra Kelman, Mayor Sharon Pratt Kelly, Robert Kemp, Beb Kelter, Rashon Khan, Joan Logue Kinder, Woodie King Jr., Ken Knuckles, Vallery Kountze, Diane Lacey, Cyndi LaMonica, Stan Lathan, Leonard Lee, Michael Levine, Jerry Lewis, Grace Liccione, Fran Lipson, Bowlegged Lou, Mary Major, Wynton Marsalis, Tim Marshall, Carol Martin, Joel Martin, Michael Mauldin, Kim Mayner, James McBride, Carl McCaskill, Scooter McCray, Mike McDermott, Deborah McDuffie, Genevieve Michel, Alan Mirabella, Grace Mirabella, Mark Monteverdi, Moet, Marie Moore, Joy Thomas Moore, Anthony Morcone, Allen Morgan, Joan Morgan, Paul A. Moses, Dick Munro, Andy Murcia, Ray Murphy Jr., Jim Murray, Hakim Mutlag, Kia Neal, Hope Newton, Susan Nowak, Carolyn Odom, Lela Ward Oliver, Robert Osbourne, Jean Owensby, Patrick Pacheco, Betty Patel, Richard Parsons, Basil Paterson, Jerome Patterson, Gerald Peart, Frances Pennington, Pennington School Family: (The Selwyns, Weisses, Remers, Geists), Richard Plepler, Gwen Pointer, Melanie Procter, Regine Radford, George Raveling, Rosemary Ravinal, Lisa Ray, Tracy Richards, Matty Rich, William Richardson, Carrie Robinson, Nina Robinson, Faye and Karl Rodney, Charles Rogers, Ron Rogers, Howard Rubenstein, Reginald Rutherford, Ruby Ryles, John Salley, Patrick Savin, Saxton's Barber Shop Crew (Tim, Russell, Mike, Mike, and Cliff), Mitch Schneider, Jean Way Schoonover, Dick Scott, Judith Service, Pat Shields, Peter Shukat, Sue Simmons, Russell Simmons, Pam Sims, Sinbad, The Singer Family, Karen Singletary, Sydney Small, Mary Smalls, Judy Smith, Patricia Smith, Wayne Sobers, Paula Span, Lonnie Stafford, Juanita Stephens, Chris Suter, Percy Sutton, Barry Talesnick, Don Thomas, Karen Thomas, Isiah Thomas, Art

Thompson, Robert Townsend, Brenda Trotter, Artie Tullman, Arnold Turner, Cicely Tyson, Oscar Upchurch, Michael Vann, Michael Wallach, Cheryl Washington, Ken Webb, Harvey Weinstein, DeWayne Wickham, Oprah Winfrey, Leah Wilcox, Bruce Williams, Dick Williams, Elaine Williams, Lena Williams, Montel Williams, Teri R. C. Williams, Jeannie Williams, Ray Williams, Roz Williams, Valerie Williams, Dave and Tonya Winfield, Ronnie Wright, Leon Wynter, Sam Yanes, Paul and Gaylord Yizar.

For those who have passed on . . . your spirit will live in me forever:

Bert Andrews, Arthur Ashe, Debbie Butler Clark, Miles Davis, D. Parke Gibson, Clarence Hunter, Vickie Klein, Charlie Napoli, Staunton Perkins, Jonathan Schenker, Morris Warren.

I know you're probably thinking, she must have listed everyone she ever knew!! But this isn't even close—these are just a few of the near and dear. And if, by some remote chance, I have omitted anyone, please forgive me. I'll catch you on the next chapter.